Contents

Copyright © McDougal Littell/Houghton Mifflin Company.

Copyright © McDougal Littell/Houghton Mifflin Company.

McDougal Littell

ECONOMICS
Concepts and Choices

Standards–Based Assessment

McDougal Littell
A HOUGHTON MIFFLIN COMPANY
Evanston, Illinois • Boston • Dallas

Warning: Permission is hereby granted to teachers to reprint or photocopy in classroom quantities the pages or sheets in this work that carry the following copyright notice: Copyright © McDougal Littell/Houghton Mifflin Company. These pages are designed to be reproduced by teachers for use in their classes with accompanying McDougal Littell material, provided each copy made shows the copyright notice. Such copies may not be sold, and further distribution is expressly prohibited. Except as authorized above, prior written permission must be obtained from McDougal Littell to reproduce or transmit this work or portions thereof in any other form or by any electronic or mechanical means, including any information storage or retrieval system, unless expressly permitted by federal copyright law. Address inquiries to Supervisor, Rights and Permissions, McDougal Littell, P.O. Box 1667, Evanston, IL 60204.

ISBN-10: 0–618–88714–8

ISBN 978-0-618-88714-9

Copyright © McDougal Littell, a division of Houghton Mifflin Company. All rights reserved.

6 7 8 9 -2266- 13

4500412815

Copyright © McDougal Littell/Houghton Mifflin Company.

To the Teacher

The Standards-Based Assessment Book includes three key elements to help you identify what your students need to learn, to assess how well they understand basic economics concepts, and to provide students with extra help if they need it.

1. **National Council on Economic Education National Content Standards in Economics:** These standards provide a framework for the study of economics used in schools across the country. They identify the fundamental ideas, relationships, and patterns that students need to learn in a high school economics course.

2. **Standards-Based Unit Tests:** Each test consists of 25 multiple-choice items, and includes one or more charts, graphs, or other exhibits. Items assess student understanding of the core content presented in each unit of the pupil's book. The standards covered in each test are listed below.
   - **Unit 1:** Standards 1, 2, 3, 14, 16
   - **Unit 2:** Standards 2, 7, 8, 9, 16
   - **Unit 3:** Standards 9, 10, 13, 16
   - **Unit 4:** Standards 4, 8, 10, 11, 12
   - **Unit 5:** Standards 15, 18, 19
   - **Unit 6:** Standards 12, 16, 20
   - **Unit 7:** Standards 5, 6, 11, 15, 16

3. **Reteaching Activities:** Reproducible black-line master worksheets provide students with additional practice in reviewing and understanding the key information presented in each section.

Copyright © McDougal Littell/Houghton Mifflin Company.

National Council on Economic Education National Content Standards in Economics

Standard 1: Scarcity

Students will understand that:

Productive resources are limited. Therefore, people can not have all the goods and services they want; as a result, they must choose some things and give up others.

Students will be able to use this knowledge to:

Identify what they gain and what they give up when they make choices.

Standard 2: Marginal Cost/Benefit

Students will understand that:

Effective decision making requires comparing the additional costs of alternatives with the additional benefits. Most choices involve doing a little more or a little less of something: few choices are "all or nothing" decisions.

Students will be able to use this knowledge to:

Make effective decisions as consumers, producers, savers, investors, and citizens.

Standard 3: Allocation of Goods and Services

Students will understand that:

Different methods can be used to allocate goods and services. People acting individually or collectively through government must choose which methods to use to allocate different kinds of goods and services.

Students will be able to use this knowledge to:

Evaluate different methods of allocating goods and services by comparing the benefits and costs of each method.

Standard 4: Role of Incentives

Students will understand that:

People respond predictably to positive and negative incentives.

Students will be able to use this knowledge to:

Identify incentives that affect people's behavior and explain how incentives affect their own behavior.

Standard 5: Gain from Trade

Students will understand that:

Voluntary exchange occurs only when all participating parties expect to gain. This is true for trade among individuals or organizations within a nation, and among individuals or organizations in different nations.

Students will be able to use this knowledge to:

Negotiate exchanges and identify the gains to themselves and others. Compare the benefits and costs of policies that alter trade barriers between nations, such as tariffs and quotas.

Standard 6: Specialization and Trade

Students will understand that:

When individuals, regions, and nations specialize in what they can produce at the lowest cost and then trade with others, both production and consumption increase.

Students will be able to use this knowledge to:

Explain how they can benefit themselves and others by developing special skills and strengths.

Copyright © McDougal Littell/Houghton Mifflin Company.

Standard 7: Markets—Price and Quantity Determination

Students will understand that:

Markets exist when buyers and sellers interact. This interaction determines market prices and thereby allocates scarce goods and services.

Students will be able to use this knowledge to:

Identify markets in which they have participated as a buyer and as a seller and describe how the interaction of all buyers and sellers influences prices. Also, predict how prices change when there is either a shortage or surplus of the product available.

Standard 8: Role of Price in Market System

Students will understand that:

Prices send signals and provide incentives to buyers and sellers. When supply or demand changes, market prices adjust, affecting incentives.

Students will be able to use this knowledge to:

Predict how prices change when the number of buyers or sellers in a market changes, and explain how the incentives facing individual buyers and sellers are affected.

Standard 9: Role of Competition

Students will understand that:

Competition among sellers lowers costs and prices, and encourages producers to produce more of what consumers are willing and able to buy. Competition among buyers increases prices and allocates goods and services to those people who are willing and able to pay the most for them.

Students will be able to use this knowledge to:

Explain how changes in the level of competition in different markets can affect them.

Standard 10: Role of Economic Institutions

Students will understand that:

Institutions evolve in market economies to help individuals and groups accomplish their goals. Banks, labor unions, corporations, legal systems, and not-for-profit organizations are examples of important institutions. A different kind of institution, clearly defined and enforced property rights, is essential to a market economy.

Students will be able to use this knowledge to:

Describe the roles of various economic institutions.

Standard 11: Role of Money

Students will understand that:

Money makes it easier to trade, borrow, save, invest, and compare the value of goods and services.

Students will be able to use this knowledge to:

Explain how their lives would be more difficult in a world with no money, or in a world where money sharply lost its value.

Copyright © McDougal Littell/Houghton Mifflin Company.

Standard 12: Role of Interest Rates

Students will understand that:

Interest rates, adjusted for inflation, rise and fall to balance the amount saved with the amount borrowed, which affects the allocation of scarce resources between present and future uses.

Students will be able to use this knowledge to:

Explain situations in which they pay or receive interest, and explain how they would react to changes in interest rates if they were making or receiving interest payments.

Standard 13: Role of Resources in Determining Income

Students will understand that:

Income for most people is determined by the market value of the productive resources they sell. What workers earn depends, primarily, on the market value of what they produce and how productive they are.

Students will be able to use this knowledge to:

Predict future earnings based on their current plans for education, training, and career options.

Standard 14: Profit and the Entrepreneur

Students will understand that:

Entrepreneurs are people who take the risks of organizing productive resources to make goods and services. Profit is an important incentive that leads entrepreneurs to accept the risks of business failure.

Students will be able to use this knowledge to:

Identify the risks, returns, and other characteristics of entrepreneurship that bear on its attractiveness as a career.

Standard 15: Growth

Students will understand that:

Investment in factories, machinery, new technology, and in the health, education, and training of people can raise future standards of living.

Students will be able to use this knowledge to:

Predict the consequences of investment decisions made by individuals, businesses, and governments.

Standard 16: Role of Government

Students will understand that:

There is an economic role for government in a market economy whenever the benefits of a government policy outweigh its costs. Governments often provide for national defense, address environmental concerns, define and protect property rights, and attempt to make markets more competitive. Most government policies also redistribute income.

Students will be able to use this knowledge to:

Identify and evaluate the benefits and costs of alternative public policies, and assess who enjoys the benefits and who bears the costs.

Standard 17: Using Cost/Benefit Analysis to Evaluate Government Programs

Students will understand that:

Costs of government policies sometimes exceed benefits. This may occur because of incentives facing voters, government officials, and government employees, because of actions by special interest groups that can impose costs on the general public, or because social goals other than economic efficiency are being pursued.

Copyright © McDougal Littell/Houghton Mifflin Company.

Students will be able to use this knowledge to:

Identify some public policies that may cost more than the benefits they generate, and assess who enjoys the benefits and who bears the costs. Explain why the policies exist.

Standard 18: Macroeconomy— Income/Employment, Prices

Students will understand that:

A nation's overall levels of income, employment, and prices are determined by the interaction of spending and production decisions made by all households, firms, government agencies, and others in the economy.

Students will be able to use this knowledge to:

Interpret media reports about current economic conditions and explain how these conditions can influence decisions made by consumers, producers, and government policy makers.

Standard 19: Unemployment and Inflation

Students will understand that:

Unemployment imposes costs on individuals and nations. Unexpected inflation imposes costs on many people and benefits some others because it arbitrarily redistributes purchasing power. Inflation can reduce the rate of growth of national living standards because individuals and organizations use resources to protect themselves against the uncertainty of future prices.

Students will be able to use this knowledge to:

Make informed decisions by anticipating the consequences of inflation and unemployment.

Standard 20: Monetary and Fiscal Policy

Students will understand that:

Federal government budgetary policy and the Federal Reserve System's monetary policy influence the overall levels of employment, output, and prices.

Students will be able to use this knowledge to:

Anticipate the impact of federal government and Federal Reserve System macroeconomic policy decisions on themselves and others.

Copyright © McDougal Littell/Houghton Mifflin Company.

UNIT 1

UNIT BENCHMARK TEST

Economics and Choice

Part 1: Main Ideas

Choose the letter of the best answer. (4 points each)

_____ 1. 1. Scarcity is a problem because of the tension between limited resources and unlimited

    a. choice

    b. goods

    c. needs

    d. wants

_____ 2. As a factor of production, capital means

    a. human-made resources used for business purposes

    b. money used for business purposes

    c. natural resources used for business purposes

    d. stocks sold for business purposes

_____ 3. The term for the value of the next best alternative in an economic decision is

    a. cost-benefit analysis

    b. free lunch

    c. opportunity cost

    d. trade off

_____ 4. If you decide to buy a $25 sweater rather than a $20 sweater, your marginal cost is

    a. $5

    b. $15

    c. $20

    d. $25

_____ 5. An outward shift in a production possibilities curve could be caused by

    a. fewer resources available

    b. more resources available

    c. underutilization

    d. efficiency

_____ 6. Adam Smith's "invisible hand" works only in a

    a. command economy

    b. market economy

    c. planned economy

    d. traditional economy

_____ 7. People are most likely to agree on economic goals and roles in a

    a. command economy

    b. market economy

    c. planned economy

    d. traditional economy

_____ 8. According to Karl Marx, all of human history has been a struggle between

    a. consumers and producers

    b. government and business

    c. upper and lower classes

    d. factory workers and farmers

Copyright © McDougal Littell/Houghton Mifflin Company.

9. In Marx's view, the factory owner's profit depends upon

   a. an efficient approach to the use of natural resources
   b. the degree of competition from other producers
   c. a favorable political climate
   d. the use of human labor as a commodity

10. In a command economy, the government

   a. encourages entrepreneurs
   b. controls basic industries
   c. regulates the stock market
   d. protects private property

11. North Korea's economic problems stem mainly from

   a. prolonged drought
   b. misguided central planning
   c. out of date farming methods
   d. unrestricted free markets

12. The type of government most often associated with a command economy is a(n)

   a. authoritarian regime
   b. democracy
   c. federation
   d. monarchy

13. Private property rights are important in a market economy because they

   a. are vital to any sale or exchange
   b. determine price levels
   c. encourage people to be generous
   d. let the government know whom to tax

14. One fundamental of a market economy is

   a. consumer sovereignty
   b. high taxes
   c. government-controlled factories
   d. national health insurance

15. The United States has

   a. laissez faire capitalism
   b. laissez faire socialism
   c. a modified command economy
   d. a modified capitalist economy

16. The American Motor Company's decision to stop manufacturing the Gremlin automobile can best be described as an example of

   a. competition
   b. consumer sovereignty
   c. specialization
   d. voluntary exchange

Copyright © McDougal Littell/Houghton Mifflin Company.

_____ **17.** Customers of the factor markets are

    a. businesses

    b. households

    c. individuals

    d. workers

_____ **18.** In the circular flow model, money flows

    a. one way and business revenue flows another

    b. one way and products flow another

    c. the same way as goods and services

    d. the same way as productive resources

_____ **19.** Of the following nations, the country with a mixed economy that leans most toward socialism is

    a. France

    b. Namibia

    c. Sweden

    d. the United States

_____ **20.** As a country goes through a transition from a command to a market economy, it is most likely to

    a. decrease global ties

    b. establish price controls

    c. nationalize key industries

    d. privatize industries

_____ **21.** A person who lives downstream from a polluting factory may experience a

    a. free ride

    b. negative externality

    c. positive externality

    d. public transfer

_____ **22.** Government programs designed to protect people from economic hardships may be best described as a

    a. free ride

    b. positive externality

    c. public good

    d. safety net

Copyright © McDougal Littell/Houghton Mifflin Company.

UNIT 1

Part 2: Interpreting Charts

Using the exhibit, choose the letter of the best answer. (4 points each)

Crop Statistics				
Region	Sorghum area (acres)	Sorghum produced (tons)	Millet area (acres)	Millet produced (tons)
Africa	65,729,073	24,893,718	50,976,483	15,626,629
Asia	27,680,763	12,130,345	35,688,515	14,602,258
Europe	407,050	644,372	1,987,168	791,447
Latin America and Caribbean	10,091,808	13,461,701	25,100	18,755
North America	5,803,250	11,005,874	521,050	337,920

Source: Food and Agriculture Organization of the United Nations, 2005

_____ 23. The region with the greatest amount of land devoted to sorghum was

    a. Africa

    b. Asia

    c. Latin America and Caribbean

    d. North America

_____ 24. The region that produced the least millet was

    a. Africa

    b. Europe

    c. Latin America and Caribbean

    d. North America

_____ 25. The region that produced the highest sorghum yield (tons per acre) was

    a. Africa

    b. Asia

    c. Latin America and Caribbean

    d. North America

Copyright © McDougal Littell/Houghton Mifflin Company.

UNIT BENCHMARK TEST

Market Economies at Work

Part 1: Main Ideas

Choose the letter of the best answer. (4 points each)

_____ 1. When the price of a good or service falls, consumers usually buy more of it. Which law does this statement reflect?

    a. demand

    b. diminishing marginal utility

    c. diminishing returns

    d. supply

_____ 2. Sometimes consumers buy less of one product because they buy a similar product at a lower price. What pattern of behavior does this example reflect?

    a. law of demand

    b. income effect

    c. law of diminishing marginal utility

    d. substitution effect

_____ 3. When the price of a good or service falls and consumers buy more of it, what is it that has changed?

    a. consumer taste

    b. demand

    c. market size

    d. quantity demanded

_____ 4. The popularity of MP3 players led many broadcasters to begin offering podcasts of popular programs. Which factor that affects demand does this example illustrate?

    a. complements

    b. consumer income

    c. market size

    d. substitutes

_____ 5. Which statement about the reasons for gasoline's inelastic demand is true?

    a. Gasoline does not follow the law of demand.

    b. Gasoline has no close substitutes.

    c. Gasoline is a luxury for most households.

    d. Gasoline takes a large part of the average income.

_____ 6. Which of these signals and incentives do shortages provide?

    a. It is a good time for consumers to buy as prices fall.

    b. It is a good time for producers to raise prices.

    c. It is time for producers to leave the market.

    d. Prices are too high relative to consumer demand.

_____ 7. Which situations cause equilibrium price to rise? I The number of buyers decreases. II The number of buyers increases. III The number of sellers decreases. IV The number of sellers increases.

    a. I and III   **c.** II and III

    b. I and IV   **d.** II and IV

_____ 8. Which is a result of rent control?

    a. More new affordable housing is built.

    b. The quality of housing improves.

    c. Tenants are forced to move frequently.

    d. There is a persistent shortage of housing.

Copyright © McDougal Littell/Houghton Mifflin Company.

9. Which term applies to the minimum wage?

   a. black market

   b. price ceiling

   c. price floor

   d. rationing

10. Producers are willing to sell more goods and services at higher prices than at lower prices. Which law does this statement reflect?

    a. demand

    b. diminishing marginal utility

    c. increasing returns

    d. supply

11. Higher prices provide an incentive for producers to sell more goods and services because producers need to

    a. cover their higher costs of production

    b. increase their market share

    c. meet higher demand for their products

    d. sell to a bigger market

12. A business experiences negative returns when the hiring of new workers causes total

    a. costs to decrease

    b. costs to increase rapidly

    c. output to decrease

    d. output to increase slowly

13. Profit maximizing output occurs when marginal cost equals

    a. marginal product

    b. marginal revenue

    c. total revenue

    d. variable cost

14. If the price of apples falls from $2 per pound to $1 per pound, the Jones family brings half as many pounds to sell at the farmer's market. This example shows a change in

    a. costs of production

    b. market size

    c. quantity supplied

    d. supply

15. If the higher price of milk causes the supply of ice cream to decrease, the change in supply is due to

    a. government action

    b. input costs

    c. number of producers

    d. productivity

16. Growth of the Internet allowed mail order clothing companies to increase the amount of clothing they sold. This change in supply was due to

    a. government action

    b. number of producers

    c. producer price expectations

    d. technology

Copyright © McDougal Littell/Houghton Mifflin Company.

_____ **17.** The market structures with large numbers of buyers and sellers are

   a. monopolistic competition and oligopoly

   b. monopolistic competition and perfect competition

   c. monopoly and oligopoly

   d. oligopoly and perfect competition

_____ **18.** The distinguishing characteristics of monopolistic competition are

   a. few sellers and significant control of prices

   b. informed buyers and standardized products

   c. price making and restricted markets

   d. product differentiation and nonprice competition

_____ **19.** The market structures that are most likely to use advertising as a way to compete for customers are

   a. monopolistic competition and oligopoly

   b. monopolistic competition and perfect competition

   c. monopoly and oligopoly

   d. oligopoly and perfect competition

_____ **20.** A monopoly in which a single supplier is the most efficient way to provide a good or service is a

   a. geographic monopoly

   b. government monopoly

   c. natural monopoly

   d. technological monopoly

_____ **21.** When the government grants a company a patent for a product or service it is

   a. encouraging increased competition

   b. establishing a government monopoly

   c. protecting the company's property rights

   d. protecting consumers from unsafe products

_____ **22.** An illegal business practice designed to drive competitors out of business is

   a. a cease and desist order

   b. a deceptive advertising campaign

   c. predatory pricing

   d. price discrimination

Copyright © McDougal Littell/Houghton Mifflin Company.

UNIT 2

Part 2: Interpreting Graphs

Using the exhibit, chose the letter of the best answer. (4 points each)

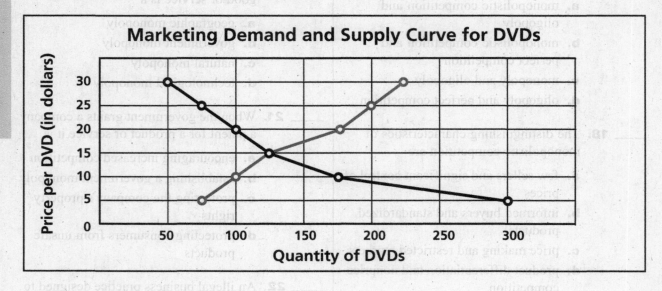

Marketing Demand and Supply Curve for DVDs

_____ **23.** What is the equilibrium price shown on the graph?

    a. $10

    b. $15

    c. $20

    d. $25

_____ **24.** Based on the graph, which statement describes the situation at equilibrium price?

    a. Quantity demanded and quantity supplied are equal.

    b. Quantity demanded is at its greatest amount.

    c. Quantity demanded is greater than quantity supplied.

    d. Quantity supplied is at its greatest amount.

_____ **25.** What happens when the price is $20 per DVD?

    a. Quantity demanded and quantity supplied are equal.

    b. Quantity demanded is greater than quantity supplied.

    c. There is a shortage of 75 DVDs.

    d. There is a surplus of 75 DVDs.

Copyright © McDougal Littell/Houghton Mifflin Company.

UNIT 3

UNIT BENCHMARK TEST

Partners in the American Economy

Part 1: Main Ideas

Choose the letter of the best answer. (4 points each)

_____ 1. The most common type of business organization in the United States is the

   a. corporation
   b. franchise
   c. general partnership
   d. sole proprietorship

_____ 2. The percentage of U.S. business sales generated by sole proprietorships is

   a. 5%
   b. 10%
   c. 25%
   d. 75%

_____ 3. The type of business organization that has the greatest access to resources is the

   a. cooperative
   b. corporation
   c. general partnership
   d. nonprofit organization

_____ 4. Cocoa-nuts, a business that sells chocolates and a variety of nuts, has independently owned shops throughout the nation. Cocoa-nuts is a

   a. cooperative
   b. conglomerate
   c. franchise
   d. merger

_____ 5. One of the major disadvantages of corporations is

   a. double taxation
   b. limited liability
   c. limited life
   d. over specialization

_____ 6. Stockholders in a corporation are at risk of losing

   a. dividends
   b. personal savings
   c. the right to profits earned
   d. the value of their investment

_____ 7. The merger of two corporations that both provide telephone services is best described as a

   a. horizontal merger
   b. layered merger
   c. multinational merger
   d. vertical merger

_____ 8. A merger of a mining corporation and a company that manufactures mining equipment is called a

   a. cooperative merger
   b. conglomerate merger
   c. horizontal merger
   d. vertical merger

Copyright © McDougal Littell/Houghton Mifflin Company.

UNIT 3

9. Corporations and nonprofit organizations both have

   a. a board of directors
   b. double taxation
   c. limited liability
   d. a large number of stockholders

10. In a limited liability partnership,

   a. all of the partners have unlimited liability
   b. at least one partner has unlimited liability
   c. two or more have unlimited liability
   d. none of the partners has unlimited liability

11. In a limited liability partnership, partners are responsible for

   a. nothing beyond their investment
   b. the debts and mistakes of all other partners
   c. the mistakes of all other partners
   d. their own mistakes

12. At the equilibrium wage, the

   a. demand for workers is greater than the supply
   b. demand for workers is increasing
   c. supply and demand of workers are equal
   d. supply is greater than the demand

13. If the hourly wage for technical support representatives falls from $15 to $13, the demand for technical support representatives will

   a. decrease
   b. increase
   c. reach equilibrium
   d. stay the same

14. If the hourly wage for technical support representatives rises from $15 to $18, the supply of technical support representatives will

   a. decrease
   b. increase
   c. reach equilibrium
   d. stay the same

15. Legislation that has had a direct impact on wages is the

   a. Civil Rights Act
   b. Norris-LaGuardia Act
   c. Taft-Hartley Act
   d. Wagner Act

16. Organized labor in the United States helped to establish

   a. collective bargaining
   b. contingent employment
   c. stock options
   d. executive bonuses

Copyright © McDougal Littell/Houghton Mifflin Company.

UNIT 3

_____ **17.** The segment of the labor market that has grown the most since the mid-1950s is

   a. college graduates

   b. high school graduates

   c. women

   d. workers

_____ **18.** The word that best describes today's labor market is

   a. global

   b. local

   c. national

   d. regional

_____ **19.** Unions organized according to the skills of member workers are called

   a. craft unions

   b. federated unions

   c. industrial unions

   d. progressive unions

_____ **20.** A key victory of the CIO was unionizing the workers at

   a. Carnegie Steel

   b. Ford Motor Company

   c. McCormick Harvester

   d. Pullman Palace Car Company

_____ **21.** In a march to the home of President Theodore Roosevelt, labor activist Mary Harris Jones focused attention on the treatment of

   a. African American workers

   b. child laborers

   c. coal miners

   d. women workers

_____ **22.** All of the following help explain the decline of unions in the late 20th century EXCEPT

   a. cases of union corruption

   b. right-to-work laws

   c. SEIU's departure from the AFL-CIO

   d. the shift from manufacturing to service industries

Copyright © McDougal Littell/Houghton Mifflin Company.

UNIT 3

Part 2: Interpreting Charts

Using the exhibits, choose the letter of the best answer. (4 points each)

Organization A

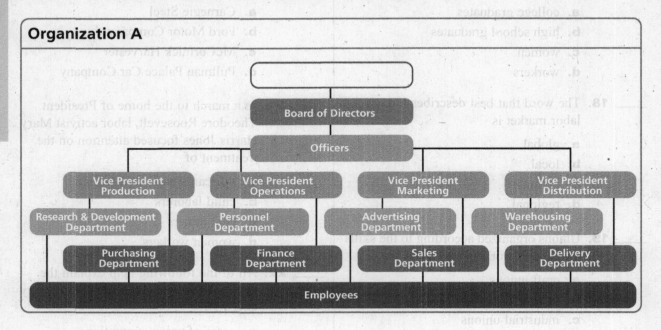

_____ **23.** Organization A is a
    a. partnership
    b. franchise
    c. corporation
    d. conglomerate

_____ **24.** The blank space in the structural chart for Organization A should be marked as
    a. franchisees
    b. officers
    c. partners
    d. stockholders

_____ **25.** One advantage of Organization A is that it
    a. has unlimited liability
    b. has unlimited life
    c. is not expensive to start up
    d. is not heavily regulated

Copyright © McDougal Littell/Houghton Mifflin Company.

UNIT
4

UNIT BENCHMARK TEST

Money, Banking, and Finance

Part 1: Main Ideas

Choose the letter of the best answer. (4 points each)

_____ 1. What do you call anything that people will accept as payment for goods and services?
- **a.** bonds
- **b.** money
- **c.** savings
- **d.** stocks

_____ 2. Which physical property of money allows sellers to make change?
- **a.** divisibility
- **b.** durability
- **c.** portability
- **d.** uniformity

_____ 3. Which physical property of money explains why representative money replaced commodity money such as gold and silver?
- **a.** divisibility
- **b.** durability
- **c.** portability
- **d.** uniformity

_____ 4. Which economic property of money refers to its use as a medium of exchange?
- **a.** acceptability
- **b.** portability
- **c.** scarcity
- **d.** stability

_____ 5. Which function of money makes it easier for people to save their money to spend in the future?
- **a.** medium of exchange
- **b.** standard of value
- **c.** store of value
- **d.** uniformity of currency

_____ 6. Which function of money allows you to decide if you want to buy two $10 movie tickets or a $20 DVD?
- **a.** medium of exchange
- **b.** standard of value
- **c.** store of value
- **d.** uniformity of currency

_____ 7. Which of the following is NOT part of M1?
- **a.** checking account deposits
- **b.** coins
- **c.** paper money
- **d.** savings account deposits

_____ 8. Which statement best describes the original purpose of savings and loan associations?
- **a.** to allow the government to deposit tax receipts
- **b.** to allow savers to borrow money for homes
- **c.** to make loans to businesses
- **d.** to provide investment advice

Copyright © McDougal Littell/Houghton Mifflin Company.

UNIT 4

_____ **9.** Which of the following makes credit unions different from other banks?

   a. automobile loans

   b. checking accounts

   c. home mortgages

   d. membership requirements

_____ **10.** Which of these products does NOT allow people a way to save money and earn interest?

   a. certificate of deposit

   b. home mortgage

   c. money market account

   d. savings account

_____ **11.** Which of the following allows banks to create money by making loans?

   a. bank mergers

   b. deregulation

   c. electronic banking

   d. fractional reserve banking

_____ **12.** Which of these cards provides an easy way for you to borrow money?

   a. ATM

   b. credit

   c. debit

   d. stored value

_____ **13.** An example of a nonbank financial intermediary is a

   a. commercial bank

   b. credit union

   c. insurance company

   d. savings and loan association

_____ **14.** A financial intermediary that pools funds from many investors to purchase a range of financial assets for them is a

   a. finance company

   b. insurance company

   c. mutual fund

   d. pension fund

_____ **15.** Compound interest provides an additional incentive to save because

   a. interest rates are guaranteed to increase every year

   b. interest is applied to accumulated interest as well as the initial deposit

   c. the amount of interest doubles each year

   d. banks pay higher interest rates for longer term investments

_____ **16.** As a means to save for emergencies, money market accounts offer the benefit of

   a. increasing in value over time

   b. liquidity

   c. locking in funds for a period of time

   d. tax-free earnings

Copyright © McDougal Littell/Houghton Mifflin Company.

_____ **17.** In order to get the highest possible return on their investments, investors take on the greater risk of investing in

 a. insured savings accounts

 b. certificates of deposit

 c. stocks and corporate bonds

 d. Treasury bills

_____ **18.** Investors who put all their money in investments with a guaranteed return still face the risk of

 a. corporations declaring bankruptcy

 b. economic factors affecting the value of stock

 c. losing purchasing power from inflation

 d. losing some of their principal

_____ **19.** A financial market where securities are bought and sold is a

 a. savings bank

 b. finance company

 c. insurance company

 d. stock exchange

_____ **20.** Corporations offer investors a share of ownership in the corporation through

 a. savings bonds

 b. certificates of deposit

 c. money market mutual funds

 d. money market mutual funds

Copyright © McDougal Littell/Houghton Mifflin Company.

UNIT 4

Part 2: Interpreting Graphs

Using the graph, choose the letter of the best idea. (4 points each)

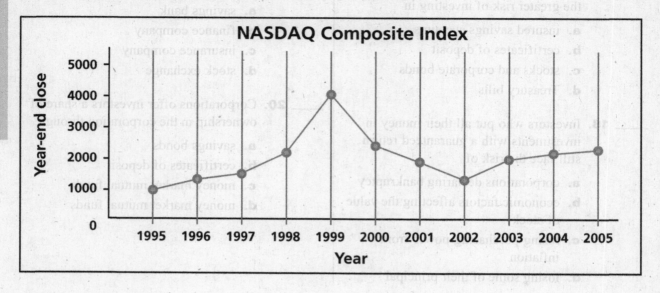

NASDAQ Composite Index

21. Between 1995 and 1999, the prices of stocks on the NASDAQ market provided an incentive to people to

   a. buy stocks at bargain prices
   b. sell stocks for a profit
   c. turn to other investments for better returns
   d. view stocks as a safe investment

22. Based on the graph, demand for stocks on the NASDAQ market were lowest in

   a. 2001
   b. 2002
   c. 2003
   d. 2004

23. Investors who purchase bonds because they want the guaranteed interest income will be most concerned with

   a. liquidity
   b. maturity
   c. par value
   d. yield

24. The type of bond that carries the highest risk and the highest yield is a

   a. junk bond
   b. municipal bond
   c. savings bond
   d. Treasury bond

25. Bond investors who want to sell their bonds before the maturity date in order to make a profit would sell when the

   a. bond rating has declined
   b. coupon rate has risen
   c. par value has fallen
   d. yield has fallen

Copyright © McDougal Littell/Houghton Mifflin Company.

UNIT BENCHMARK TEST

Measuring and Monitoring Economic Performance

Part 1: Main Ideas

Choose the letter of the best answer. (4 points each)

_____ 1. In the formula for determining Gross Domestic Product (C+I+G+X=GDP), X stands for

    a. exports

    b. external sales

    c. gross exports

    d. net exports

_____ 2. To find nominal GDP, economists calculate GDP in

    a. comparison to a base year

    b. the current year's dollars

    c. the dollars of the year 2000

    d. comparison to the population

_____ 3. GDP is an especially good estimate of

    a. nonmarket activities

    b. quality of life

    c. the economy's performance

    d. the mix of products and services

_____ 4. To calculate per capita income, economists use

    a. disposable personal income

    b. national income

    c. national income minus disposable personal income

    d. personal income

_____ 5. During the contraction phase of the business cycle,

    a. prices rise

    b. resources become less scarce

    c. resources become more scarce

    d. unemployment declines

_____ 6. The aggregate supply curve is almost horizontal when real GDP is low because businesses

    a. are reluctant to raise prices

    b. increase their workers' wages

    c. reduce their workers' wages

    d. try to earn more by raising prices

_____ 7. Falling interest rates will lead to

    a. decreased aggregate demand

    b. decreased spending

    c. increased aggregate demand

    d. increased savings

_____ 8. The Great Depression came to an end when

    a. bank failures stopped

    b. New Deal legislation went into effect

    c. the government cut back spending

    d. the United States entered World War II

Copyright © McDougal Littell/Houghton Mifflin Company.

UNIT 5

9. Economic growth depends on

   a. building up the national treasury

   b. efficient and productive use of resources

   c. exporting more than importing

   d. growing populations

10. One factor that may not be essential for economic growth is

   a. capital deepening

   b. human capital

   c. natural resources

   d. technology and innovation

11. The predictions of Thomas Malthus did not come true because

   a. agricultural productivity kept pace with population growth

   b. he failed to foresee the costs of economic growth

   c. agricultural productivity did not increase as quickly as he thought

   d. population grew more quickly than he anticipated

12. The type of unemployment that can be a sign of a healthy economy is

   a. cyclical unemployment

   b. frictional unemployment

   c. seasonal unemployment

   d. structural unemployment

13. Those hardest hit by unemployment are

   a. females

   b. males

   c. the elderly

   d. the least experienced

14. The poverty threshold was first developed by figuring out the cost of nutritionally sound food and multiplying by

   a. two   c. four

   b. three   d. five

15. From 2000 to 2004, the poverty rate in the United States

   a. doubled

   b. dropped

   c. increased

   d. remained the same

16. A demographic change that has increased the poverty rate is the

   a. increase in immigration

   b. greater number of single-parent families

   c. greater number of women working

   d. decrease in births to unmarried mothers

17. The best description of income distribution in the United States is that the

   a. highest quintile earns about 50 percent of the income

   b. highest quintile earns about 90 percent of the income

   c. lowest quintile earns about 20 percent of the income

   d. lowest two quintiles earn about 40 percent of the income

18. When prices rose at a rate of about 322 percent per month in Germany in the 1920s, the German economy experienced

   a. creeping inflation

   b. deflation

   c. galloping inflation

   d. hyperinflation

Copyright © McDougal Littell/Houghton Mifflin Company.

UNIT 5

_____ **19.** To make sure it is as accurate as possible, the "market basket" on which the Consumer Price Index is based is

  a. adjusted online every day
  b. changed every month
  c. interchangeable with the goods in the producer price index
  d. weighted to reflect real spending

_____ **20.** With demand-pull inflation, prices rise because of

  a. a surplus of products and services
  b. falling interest rates
  c. new products and resources
  d. the scarcity of products and services

_____ **21.** Suppose you had $5,000 set aside for travel every summer for the next five years. You plan to spend $1,000 a year on your trips. However, inflation is 2 percent a year. By the fifth year, to buy what you were able to buy with the first year's $1,000, you would need about

  a. $1,020 **c.** $1,080
  b. $1,040 **d.** $1,120

Part 2: Interpreting Documents

Using the exhibit, choose the letter of the best answer. (4 points each)

This excerpt describes the economic effects of terrorist attacks on September 11, 2001.

[F]or 9/11 to affect the economy it would have had to have affected the price of an important input, such as energy, or had an adverse effect on aggregate demand via such mechanisms as consumer and business confidence, [or] a financial panic.... It was initially thought that aggregate demand was seriously affected, for while the existing data showed that GDP growth was low in the first half of 2001, data published in October showed that GDP had contracted during the 3rd quarter. This led to the claim that 'The terrorist attacks pushed a weak economy over the edge into an outright recession.' We now know, based on revised data, this is not so. At the time of 9/11 the economy was in its third consecutive quarter of contraction; positive growth resumed in the 4th quarter. This would suggest that any effects from 9/11 on demand were short lived.

—From "The Economic Effects of 9/11" by Gail Makinen. Congressional Research Service, September 27, 2002.

_____ **22.** According to this report, the business cycle reached its trough in the

  a. first quarter of 2001
  b. second quarter of 2001
  c. third quarter of 2001
  d. fourth quarter of 2001

_____ **23.** The report concludes that the events of 9/11

  a. affected aggregate demand
  b. affected the prices of oil
  c. had only short-term effects
  d. pushed the economy into a recession

Copyright © McDougal Littell/Houghton Mifflin Company.

UNIT 5

Part 3: Interpreting Advertisements

Using the exhibit, choose the letter of the best answer. (4 points each)

The following text comes from an advertisement issued by the War Advertising Council during World War II.

---

7 RULES FOR PATRIOTIC AMERICANS TO REMEMBER EVERY DAY

1. Buy only what you *absolutely need*. Make the article you have last longer by proper car. Avoid waste.

2. Pay no more than ceiling prices. Buy rationed goods only by exchanging stamps. (Rationing and ceiling prices are for *your protection*.)

3. Pay willingly any taxes that your country needs. (They are the cheapest way of paying for the war.)

4. Pay off your old debts—avoid making new ones.

5. Don't ask more money for the goods you sell or for the work you do. Higher prices come out of everybody's pocket—including *yours*.

6. Establish and maintain a savings account; maintain adequate life insurance.

7. Buy all the War Bonds you can—and hold 'em!

HELP US KEEP PRICES DOWN

_____ **24.** If people followed rules 3, 6, and 7 of the "7 Rules for Patriotic Americans," the result would probably be to

    a. increase aggregate supply

    b. increase aggregate demand

    c. decrease aggregate supply

    d. decrease aggregate demand

_____ **25.** Rules 1 and 4 of the "7 Rules for Patriotic Americans" suggests that during World War II the U.S. economy experienced

    a. a wage-price spiral.

    b. cost-push inflation.

    c. demand-pull inflation.

    d. a period of hyperinflation.

Copyright © McDougal Littell/Houghton Mifflin Company.

UNIT BENCHMARK TEST

The Role of Government in the Economy

Part 1: Main Ideas

Choose the letter of the best answer. (4 points each)

_____ 1. Which statement describes a difference between public goods and those provided by the market?

    a. The price of public goods is determined by supply and demand.

    b. Private producers can restrict access to public goods.

    c. Private producers can restrict access to public goods.

    d. Public goods benefit more than one person at a time.

_____ 2. What is the relationship between taxes and public goods?

    a. People who pay higher taxes are entitled to more public goods.

    b. Public goods are the main source of tax revenue.

    c. Public goods are the main source of tax revenue.

    d. Those who benefit the most from public goods pay the highest taxes.

_____ 3. Why is it necessary for the government to supply public goods?

    a. The government can best decide who receives public goods.

    b. The number of people who want public goods is too small for the market.

    c. Only the government is large enough to provide public goods.

    d. Private producers cannot sell public goods and make a profit.

_____ 4. Taxes on cigarettes increase their price. How are cigarette taxes related to the problem of externalities?

    a. Taxes bring the price in line with the benefits of cigarettes.

    b. Taxes help cover some of the social costs of cigarettes.

    c. Taxes encourage more companies to sell cigarettes.

    d. Taxes encourage farmers to grow more tobacco.

_____ 5. Which of the following is an example of government spending that redistributes income indirectly?

    a. Food Stamps

    b. government contracts

    c. Medicare payments

    d. retirement benefits

_____ 6. What is the biggest expense for local governments?

    a. public safety

    b. public schools

    c. public utilities

    d. public welfare

Copyright © McDougal Littell/Houghton Mifflin Company.

UNIT 6

7. How does the Federal Reserve directly control the amount of money that banks create through making loans?

   a. open market operations
   b. bank closings
   c. setting the federal funds rate
   d. setting the reserve requirement

8. Which of these monetary policy actions by the Federal Reserve decreases the money supply?

   a. buying bonds on the open market
   b. lowering the discount rate
   c. lowering the reserve requirement
   d. selling bonds on the open market

9. How does the Federal Reserve change the federal funds rate?

   a. by buying and selling bonds in open market operations
   b. by changing the amount of reserves that banks must hold
   c. by changing the rate that it charges other banks when they borrow money
   d. by setting the rate that banks charge when they lend money to other banks

10. Which of these statements describes a situation when the Fed would use a contractionary monetary policy?

   a. Aggregate supply is increasing faster than the money supply.
   b. Aggregate supply is increasing faster than the money supply.
   c. The money supply is increasing faster than GDP.
   d. Unemployment is increasing faster than GDP.

11. Which of the following is a result of expansionary monetary policy?

   a. banks lend more money
   b. business investment declines
   c. unemployment increases
   d. prices decrease

12. What is the short-term effect of contractionary money policy?

   a. consumer spending increases
   b. interest rates rise
   c. prices rise
   d. unemployment falls

13. What happens when the Fed buys bonds on the open market?

   a. demand for bonds and interest rates decrease
   b. demand for bonds and interest rates increase
   c. demand for bonds decreases and interest rates increase
   d. demand for bonds increases and interest rates decrease

14. Which of the following scenarios represent fiscal and monetary policy working together?

   a. The Fed buys bonds and the government increases spending.
   b. The Fed buys bonds and the government raises taxes.
   c. The Fed sells bonds and the government cuts taxes.
   d. The Fed sells bonds and the government increases spending.

Copyright © McDougal Littell/Houghton Mifflin Company.

_____ **15.** Which of the following scenarios represent fiscal and monetary policy in conflict with one another?

    a. The Fed buys bonds and the government cuts taxes.

    b. The Fed buys bonds and the government increases spending.

    c. The Fed sells bonds and the government increases spending.

    d. The Fed sells bonds and the government raises taxes.

_____ **16.** Government decisions to use taxation and spending to influence the economy are referred to as

    a. automatic stabilizers

    b. discretionary fiscal policy

    c. monetary policy

    d. progressive taxation

_____ **17.** The goal of expansionary fiscal policy is to increase

    a. aggregate demand

    b. interest rates

    c. taxes

    d. unemployment

_____ **18.** The goal of contractionary fiscal policy is to lower

    a. interest rates

    b. prices

    c. taxes

    d. unemployment

_____ **19.** The combination of actions that is best designed to implement contractionary fiscal policy is to

    a. decrease government spending and lower taxes

    b. decrease government spending and raise taxes

    c. increase government spending and lower taxes

    d. increase government spending and raise taxes

_____ **20.** When federal revenue exceeds federal spending in a single year the result is a

    a. balanced budget

    b. budget deficit

    c. budget surplus

    d. larger national debt

_____ **21.** The largest percentage of the money borrowed by the federal government is owed to

    a. Federal Reserve banks

    b. foreign investors

    c. savings bonds holders

    d. state and local governments

_____ **22.** When government borrowing to finance deficit spending leads to higher interest rates and lower private investment, the result is the

    a. automatic stabilizer effect

    b. crowding-out effect

    c. Laffer Curve effect

    d. spending multiplier effect

Copyright © McDougal Littell/Houghton Mifflin Company.

UNIT 6

UNIT 6

Part 2: Interpreting Charts

Using the exhibit, choose the letter of the best answer. (4 points each)

Federal Spending, FY 2007 (Estimated)	
Category	Amount (billions of dollars)
Defense	549.9
Nondefense	287.1
Subtotal direct spending	**837.0**
Government social benefits	1,274.2
Grants to state and local governments	377.8
Other transfers to the rest of the world	26.4
Subtotal transfer payments	**1,678.3**
Interest payments	316.4
Subsidies	59.2
Total all spending	**2,891.0**

Source: The Office of Management and Budget

_____ **23.** Approximately what portion of direct spending is for defense?

    a. one-fifth

    b. one-half

    c. two-thirds

    d. three-fourths

_____ **24.** About what percent of federal government spending is for transfer payments?

    a. 20 percent

    b. 40 percent

    c. 60 percent

    d. 80 percent

_____ **25.** Which of these categories is greater than interest paid on government loans?

    a. grants to state and local governments

    b. nondefense spending

    c. subsidies

    d. transfer payments to foreign countries

Copyright © McDougal Littell/Houghton Mifflin Company.

UNIT
7

UNIT BENCHMARK TEST
The Global Economy

Copyright © McDougal Littell/Houghton Mifflin Company.

UNIT 7

Part 1: Main Ideas
Choose the letter of the best answer. (4 points each)

_____ **1.** Comparative advantage results when one trading nation produces something at a lower
- **a.** marginal benefit
- **b.** marginal profit
- **c.** opportunity cost
- **d.** production cost

_____ **2.** The ability of one trading nation to make a product more efficiently than another trading nation is called
- **a.** comparative advantage
- **b.** favorable balance of trade
- **c.** voluntary export restraint
- **d.** absolute advantage

_____ **3.** International trade benefits only nations that
- **a.** export more than they import
- **b.** import more than they export
- **c.** participate in trade associations
- **d.** trade according to the law of comparative advantage

_____ **4.** If Country A decides to export some of its televisions to Country B because the market for televisions in Country A is already well satisfied, then the
- **a.** demand for televisions in Country B would decline
- **b.** demand for televisions in Country A declines
- **c.** price of televisions in Country A rises
- **d.** price of televisions in Country B rises

_____ **5.** Protective tariffs are one kind of
- **a.** embargo
- **b.** quota
- **c.** trade barrier
- **d.** trade war

_____ **6.** The effect of trade barriers on domestic industries is to
- **a.** decrease motivation for efficiency
- **b.** increase motivation for efficiency
- **c.** raise workers' pay
- **d.** subsidize imports

_____ **7.** The effect of trade barriers on domestic prices is to
- **a.** keep them stable.
- **b.** lower them.
- **c.** prevent inflation.
- **d.** raise them.

_____ **8.** When other currencies were pegged to the U.S. dollar after World War II, they were using a
- **a.** fixed rate of exchange
- **b.** flexible rate of exchange
- **c.** reciprocal rate of exchange
- **d.** trade-weighted rate of exchange

9. The value of a U.S. dollar depends today on the

   a. forces of supply and demand
   b. price of gold
   c. price of the RenMinBi
   d. value of the EU dollar

10. If one U.S. dollar buys more in France than one euro buys in the United States, then in comparison with the euro, the U.S. dollar is said to be

   a. strong
   b. surplus weighted
   c. trade weighted
   d. weak

11. With a strong U.S. dollar, American

   a. exporters benefit
   b. foreign exchange markets benefit
   c. importers benefit
   d. speculators benefit

12. The biggest customer for China's exports is

   a. India
   b. Japan
   c. Russia
   d. the United States

13. All of the following are included in NAFTA except

   a. environmental and worker protections
   b. eventual phase out of all trade barriers
   c. improved intellectual property protection
   d. unrestricted immigration among member nations

14. The World Trade Organization grew out of the recovery from

   a. the Great Depression
   b. the Suez crisis
   c. World War I
   d. World War II

15. Developed nations are characterized by a market economy, a relatively high standard of living, a high GDP, and

   a. unfavorable trade policies
   b. government corruption
   c. infrastructure difficulties
   d. widespread private property

16. Nations with a high percentage of the population working in agriculture are likely to be

   a. developed nations
   b. large energy users
   c. less developed nations
   d. transitional economies

Copyright © McDougal Littell/Houghton Mifflin Company.

_____ 17. To develop economically, nations must

    a. increase their energy use

    b. increase their energy use

    c. invent new technologies

    d. raise taxes

_____ 18. In less developed nations which were once colonies of western nations, land is often

    a. controlled by the government

    b. heavily taxed

    c. subject to expropriation

    d. transferred from state to private ownership

_____ 19. Economic and social mobility are necessary for economic development because they

    a. encourage free trade

    b. prevent government corruption

    c. provide incentive for efficiency and productivity

    d. provide incentive for dispensing privileges to favored businesses

_____ 20. When nations make a foreign portfolio investment, they

    a. establish a business in a foreign country

    b. establish a multinational business

    c. take part in foreign exchange markets

    d. take part in another nation's stock and financial markets

_____ 21. In its transition to a market economy, one of Russia's biggest problems has been

    a. corruption and insider favoritism

    b. deflation

    c. the lack of natural resources

    d. the lack of well-educated citizens

Copyright © McDougal Littell/Houghton Mifflin Company.

UNIT 7

Part 2: Interpreting Graphs

Using the exhibit, choose the letter of the best answer. (4 points each)

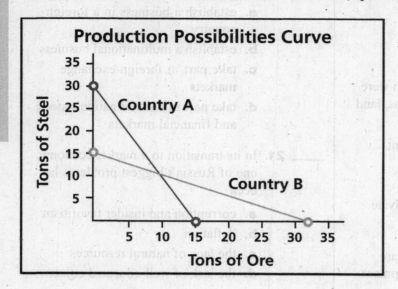

Production Possibilities Curve

Country A

Country B

Tons of Steel

Tons of Ore

_____ **22.** Country A could produce 30 tons of steel per hour if the amount of ore it produced was

a. zero
b. 5 tons
c. 10 tons
d. 15 tons

_____ **23.** The number of tons of steel Country B must give up to produce 15 tons of ore is about

a. 2.5
b. 5
c. 7.5
d. 10

_____ **24.** The steel to ore ratio for Country B is

a. .47
b. 2
c. 2.1
d. 5

_____ **25.** In terms of production of ore, Country B has

a. a comparative advantage over Country A
b. a production advantage over Country A
c. an absolute advantage over Country A
d. no advantage over Country A

Copyright © McDougal Littell/Houghton Mifflin Company.

Reteaching
Activities

Copyright © McDougal Littell/Houghton Mifflin Company.

SECTION
1

RETEACHING ACTIVITY

Scarcity: The Basic Economic Problem

A. Comparing and Contrasting Economic Terms

For each pair of terms below, tell how the terms are similar and how they are different.

1. *wants/ needs*

How they are similar _____

How they are different _____

2. *land/ capital*

How they are similar _____

How they are different _____

3. *labor/ entrepreneurship*

How they are similar _____

How they are different _____

4. *scarcity* (as an economics term)/ *scarcity* (as used in everyday speech)

How they are similar _____

How they are different _____

B. Applying Economics Concepts

As indicated on the lines below, list the three economic questions that scarcity leads to. Then give an example of how our society answers each of these questions.

5. Question 1: _____

Example: _____

6. Question 2: _____

Example: _____

7. Question 3: _____

Example: _____

Copyright © McDougal Littell/Houghton Mifflin Company.

CHAPTER 1

SECTION
2 | RETEACHING ACTIVITY
**Economic Choice Today:
Opportunity Cost**

A. Analyzing Economic Situations

For each situation, identify the incentive or utility for each option and the opportunity cost of the final choice. Write your answers on the lines provided.

1. You have the choice of two different summer jobs. Job A and job B would have you working similar hours. Both require you to work some evenings and every weekend. Job A will pay you significantly more money. Job B will give you experience that relates directly to a career you are interested in pursuing. You decide to take job B.

Incentive(s) for job A_____

Incentive(s) for job B _____

Opportunity cost of your choice_____

_____

2. You are taking your brother to a pizza restaurant. You have enough money to order one extra-large cheese pizza and two drinks or two individual pizzas of your choice and drinks. If you order the two individual pizzas, you will have enough money left to get small ice cream cones for dessert. If your order the extra large pizza, you'll have leftovers for lunch tomorrow. You decide to order the individual pizzas.

Utility of the individual pizzas_____

Utility of the extra-large pizza _____

Opportunity cost of your choice_____

_____

3. You are graduating from high school this spring. You have not done well in math. You are planning to go to the local state college in the fall. You will have to take a remedial math course. It will cost $400 to take the course at college this fall. Your high school is offering a similar course. If you pass, you won't have to take the college course. The tuition is free for the high school course. If you take the high school course, you will have to work part-time at your regular job because you will be in class in the mornings. You decide to take the course at your high school.

Incentive(s) for taking the course at your high school _____

Incentive(s) for taking the course at college_____

Utility of the high school course_____

Utility of the college course _____

Opportunity cost of your choice _____

_____

Copyright © McDougal Littell/Houghton Mifflin Company.

SECTION

3

RETEACHING ACTIVITY

Analyzing Production Possibilities

A. Analyzing Economic Data

Study the graph shown below. Answer the questions in the space provided.

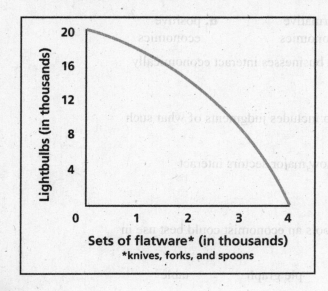

1. What oversimplified assumption does the graph make about number of types of products the society produces?

_____

2. If the society decides to make 14,000 light bulbs, how many sets of flatware can it make?

_____

3. What is the opportunity cost of increasing the number of light bulbs produced from 14,000 to 18,000?

_____

4. Mark and label a point on the graph that shows efficiency.

_____

5. Mark and label a point on the graph that shows underutilization of resources.

_____

6. If new technology made it easier to sell and distribute all sorts of housewares, including lightbulbs and flatware, what would happen to the curve?

_____

Copyright © McDougal Littell/Houghton Mifflin Company.

CHAPTER 1

SECTION

SECTION | RETEACHING ACTIVITY
4 | **The Economist's Toolbox**

A. Reviewing Economics Vocabulary

Match the definition in the first column with the term it best defines in the second column. Write the letter or your answer in the blank.

a. macroeconomics   **b.** microeconomics   **c.** normative economics   **d.** positive economics

_____ **1.** the study of how individuals, families, and businesses interact economically

_____ **2.** the study of economic behavior as it is

_____ **3.** the study of economic behavior which also includes judgments of what such behavior ought to be

_____ **4.** the study of the economy as a whole and how major sectors interact

B. Identifying Economists' Tools

Read each situation. Decide which of the following tools an economist could best use in each situation.

bar graph   economic   line graph   pie graph   table
                 model

5. An economist wants to compare the national debt of eight countries along with the percent of the gross national product (GDP) the national dept forms. _____

6. An economist wants to compare the sizes of the different spending categories that form the federal budget. _____

7. An economist wants to explain how money flows from financial institutions to industry and back to financial institutions. _____

8. An economist wants to study how the inflation rate has changed over time. _____

9. An economist wants to compare the number of doctors who work full-time in four different rural counties in a particular state. _____

10. An economist wants to show how the percentage of income that people save has dropped since the 1920s. _____

C. Summarizing the Accomplishments of an Important Economist

11. On the back of this page, summarize the ideas of Adam Smith and explain why they are important.

Copyright © McDougal Littell/Houghton Mifflin Company.

CHAPTER 2

SECTION
1

RETEACHING ACTIVITY
Introduction to Economic Systems

Comparing the Different Economic Systems

Fill in the chart to compare the different kinds of economic systems.

	Traditional Economy	Command Economy	Market Economy
Description of economic system			
Advantages			
Disadvantages			

Copyright © McDougal Littell/Houghton Mifflin Company.

CHAPTER 2

SECTION 2 | RETEACHING ACTIVITY
Command Economies

A. Identifying Command Economic Systems

Below are descriptions of how the economy runs in three imaginary countries with command economies. After reading each description, decide whether the country is a socialist country or a communist country. Circle your answer and list the features that helped you decide.

1. In this country, the government owns the all the oil wells and the processing plants used to distill petroleum and other products from the oil. Private individuals and companies own farmland, food distribution systems, and grocery stores. However, the government gives economic aid to farmers to make sure that they do not lose money producing their crops. The government also provides health-care and education for every person in the country.

   This is a (socialist/communist) country.

   Details that helped me decide:

   _____

   _____

2. In this country, the government assigns every person a career based on a test he or she takes at some point while still in school. The government owns all of the land, the factories, and the financial institutions. The government has regional directors who report to the national government. The regional directors make decisions about how to run farms, factories, banks, etc. Citizens of this country can vote for the regional directors every five years, based on how well the economy performs under their direction.

   This is a (socialist/communist) country.

   Details that helped me decide:

   _____

   _____

3. The main economic activity in this country is mining and producing aluminum. The mines and processing plants related to this industry are government-owned. Forestland and fisheries are also owned by the government. Private individuals and companies own and run the country's financial institutions, schools, and health-care system. They also own other factories, stores, and other institutions of commerce.

   This is a (socialist/communist) country.

   Details that helped me decide:

   _____

   _____

Copyright © McDougal Littell/Houghton Mifflin Company.

SECTION 3 | RETEACHING ACTIVITY
Market Economies

A. Reviewing Economic Vocabulary

Select the term that best completes each sentence. Write the term in the blank.

capitalism	product market
competition	profit
consumer sovereignty	specialization
factor market	voluntary exchange
private property rights	

1. The place where people buy and sell goods and services is called the

_____

2. Whenever two people or two sets of people make a trade in which all involved

believe that what they are getting is worth more than what they are giving up

_____ has occurred.

3. _____ occurs when people concentrate their efforts on the activities

they do best.

4. The economic system that is based on private ownership of the factors of production is

called _____

5. _____ occurs when sellers act independently to get consumers to

purchase their products.

6. The rights individuals have to own belongings, ideas, workplaces, and labor are called

_____

7. The place where people sell land, labor, capital, and entrepreneurship is called the

_____

8. The financial gain that a seller makes from a business transaction is known as

_____

9. The idea that people who purchase goods and services have ultimate control over what

gets produced because they are free to buy what they want and they do not have to buy

anything that they do not want is referred to as _____

Copyright © McDougal Littell/Houghton Mifflin Company.

CHAPTER 2

SECTION
4
RETEACHING ACTIVITY
Modern Economies in a Global Age

A. Using a Continuum to Describe Mixed Economies

Read the descriptions of the economies of the imaginary countries given below. Look at the continuum below each description. For each country, mark where you think its economy falls along the continuum and list the features of the economy that influenced your answer.

1. In this country, most people work together in family groups and go fishing and hunting to get the food that they need to survive. The government does not direct these families. However, the government owns several coal mines. It decides how much coal to produce, how much to sell to foreign governments, and how much to keep to run the power plants it owns. The government is considering developing a state-run fish cannery and having citizens work in the factory to add to government revenues.

   Traditional economy_____Command economy

   Features that helped me decide: _____

   _____

2. The government in this country provides free public education through high school for everyone. It also runs a university system that competes with private colleges. Most of the land and all industries are owned by individuals or companies. The government provides public goods, including airports, railroads, and expressways that run throughout the land.

   Market economy_____Command economy

   Features that helped me decide: _____

   _____

B. Analyzing and Evaluating Trends in Modern Economies

Answer the following questions on the back of this paper or on a separate sheet of paper.
What link exists between privatization and globalization?

4. Give three reasons why the global economy has grown in recent years. Which of these reasons do you think is the most important and why?

Copyright © McDougal Littell/Houghton Mifflin Company.

SECTION
1

RETEACHING ACTIVITY

Advantages of the Free Enterprise System

A. Reviewing Economic Vocabulary

Match the definition with the term it best defines. Write the letter of your answer in the blank next to the definition.

a. free contract
b. free enterprise system
c. legal equality
d. open opportunity
e. profit motive

_____ **1.** the ability of everyone to enter and compete in any marketplace of his or her own choosing

_____ **2.** the situation in which everyone is able to decide for himself or herself which legal agreements related to economics that they will enter into

_____ **3.** the desire of people to improve material well being by engaging in economic activities that benefit them

_____ **4.** the situation in which everyone has the same economic rights under the law

_____ **5.** capitalism

B. Identifying and Evaluating Legal Rights Under Our Economic System

6. Identify the three legal rights that are central to our economic system and rank them from most important to least important.

_____

_____

7. Explain your ranking.

_____

_____

8. What are some other factors that you think are important to allow people to succeed in our economic system? Consider legal, political, and social factors. Of the factors you listed, which do you think is most important and why?

_____

_____

Copyright © McDougal Littell/Houghton Mifflin Company.

SECTION 2

RETEACHING ACTIVITY

How Does Free Enterprise Allocate Resources?

A. Summarizing Economic Roles

Complete the chart below by summarizing how consumers, producers, and government each help allocate resources in our economic system.

Allocating Resources in the Free Enterprise System		
Consumer's Role	**Producer's Role**	**Government's Role**

B. Supporting Generalizations About our Economic System

Below are some general statements about our economic system. Read each statement. Then supply facts or examples to support each generalization.

1. Consumers vote with their wallets.

_____

_____

2. The economy of the United States is a mixed economy.

_____

_____

3. All levels of government participate in the economy.

_____

_____

4. Government is a major consumer in the U.S. economy.

_____

_____

Copyright © McDougal Littell/Houghton Mifflin Company.

SECTION 3 | RETEACHING ACTIVITY
Government and Free Enterprise

A. Reviewing Economic Vocabulary

Select the term that best completes each sentence. Write the term in the blank.

free rider	public good
infrastructure	public transfer payment
market failure	safety net
negative externality	payment
positive externality	subsidy transfer

1. The set of government programs designed to protect people from economic hardship are

referred to as a _____.

2. Someone who receives benefit from a good or service although he or she has chosen not

to pay for the good or service is called a _____.

3. The goods and services that are necessary for the smooth functioning of society are

the nation's _____.

4. A _____ occurs when people who are not part of a marketplace

interaction either benefit from the interaction or pay part of the costs.

5. If you receive money but do not provide a good or service in exchange, you have

received a _____.

6. A beneficial side effect of a transaction that affects someone other than the producer or

a buyer is called a _____.

7. Any good or service provided by the government and consumed by everyone, as a

group, is called a _____.

8. A payment made by the government to a recipient who doesn't provide any good or

service in return is called a _____.

9. A payment made by the government for part of the cost of an economic activity that will

benefit the public as a whole is called a _____.

10. A detrimental side effect of a transaction that affects someone other than the producer or

a buyer is called a _____.

Copyright © McDougal Littell/Houghton Mifflin Company.

CHAPTER 4

Copyright © McDougal Littell/Houghton Mifflin Company.

SECTION
1

RETEACHING ACTIVITY

What Is Demand?

A. Explaining Economic Concepts

Answer the questions about demand in the space provided.

1. What is demand? _____

_____

2. Restate the law of demand in your own words. _____

_____

B. Displaying Economic Data

The table below is a market demand schedule for movie tickets for a Saturday evening showing of a popular movie. Use this information to create a market demand curve for the movie tickets. Draw your curve on the grid below.

Price per Movie Ticket (in dollars)	Quantity Demanded
4.00	1,200
5.00	1,000
6.00	800
7.00	650
8.00	500
9.00	400
10.00	300
11.00	250
12.00	200
14.00	100
15.00	75
17.00	50
19.00	25

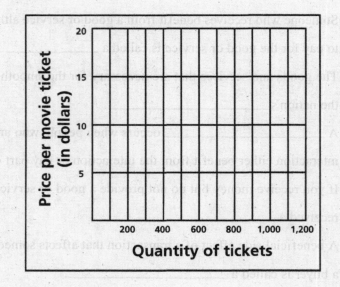

C. Analyzing and Interpreting Data

Refer to your market demand curve to answer the questions.

3. How does this demand curve illustrate the law of demand? _____

_____

4. Do you think a demand curve for movie tickets for Wednesday afternoon would differ from the demand curve you drew? Explain your answering including your reasoning. _____

_____

_____

SECTION
2

RETEACHING ACTIVITY
What Factors Affect Demand?

A. Reviewing Economic Vocabulary

Match the definition in the first column with the term it best defines in the second column. Write the letter or your answer in the blank.

a. change in demand
b. change in quantity demanded
c. complements
d. income effect
e. inferior good
f. normal goods
g. substitutes
h. substitution effect

_____ **1.** the change in the amount that consumers will buy because the purchasing power of their wages changes

_____ **2.** the change in the amount demanded because of a change in price

_____ **3.** goods and services that consumers demand more of when their incomes rise

_____ **4.** the change in the amount that consumers will buy because they buy alternate goods instead

_____ **5.** goods and services that can be used in place of each other

_____ **6.** the change that occurs when a change in the marketplace causes consumers to buy different amounts of a good or service at every price

_____ **7.** goods and services that consumers demand less of when their incomes rise

_____ **8.** goods and services that are used together, so that a rise in demand for one increases the demand for the other

B. Restating Economic Ideas

Write the answer to the question in the space provided.

Restate the law of diminishing marginal utility in your own words.

_____

_____

_____

Copyright © McDougal Littell/Houghton Mifflin Company.

CHAPTER 4

SECTION
3

RETEACHING ACTIVITY
What Is Elasticity of Demand?

A. Reviewing Economic Concepts

Answer the questions about elasticity of demand using the space provided.

1. Give definitions of the following terms:
   a. elasticity of demand

   _____

   b. elastic demand

   _____

   c. inelastic demand

   _____

   d. unit elastic

   _____

2. Describe the three factors that determine elasticity of demand.
   a.

   _____

   b.

   _____

   c.

   _____

B. Applying Economic Concepts

Answer the questions using the space provided.

3. A grocery store sold 200 bottles of laundry detergent when the price was $5.99 per bottle.
   The store sold 310 bottles of laundry detergent when the price was $3.99 per bottle.
   a. Use the space below to calculate the elasticity of demand. Is demand elastic?

   _____

   _____

   b. Use the total revenue test to figure out whether the demand for the laundry detergent
   is elastic or not. Show your work in the space below. Is demand elastic?

   _____

   _____

Copyright © McDougal Littell/Houghton Mifflin Company.

SECTION
1 | RETEACHING ACTIVITY
What Is Supply?

A. Reviewing Economic Concepts

Restate an important economic law by filling in the blanks.

1. The law of _____ states

2. that as prices rise, quantity supplied_____

3. and as prices fall, quantity supplied_____.

B. Restating and Interpreting Economic Data

Use the data from the supply curve to fill in the supply schedule. Then use the information to answer the questions.

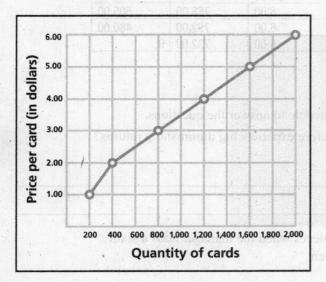

Price per Birthday Card (in dollars)	Quantity Supplied
6.00	4.
5.	6.
7.	8.
9.	10.
11.	12.
13.	200

14. How does this supply schedule for birthday cards illustrate the law of supply?

_____

_____

15. Explain why producers will supply more birthday cards at $5.00 than at $1.00.

_____

_____

Copyright © McDougal Littell/Houghton Mifflin Company.

CHAPTER 5

SECTION
2

RETEACHING ACTIVITY
What Are the Costs of Production?

A. Identifying Economic Data

Fill in the headings for the chart below, reviewing the definition of each term. Use the definitions and the other economic data to fill in the missing numbers.

Production Cost and Revenue Schedule for Party Centerpieces						
1.	2.	3. (in dollars)	4. (in dollars)	5. (in dollars)	6. (in dollars)	7. (in dollars)
0	0	30.00	—	–	0.00	−30.00
1	24	90.00	2.50	6.00	144.00	54.00
2	64	132.00	1.05	6.00	384.00	252.00
3	110	172.00	0.74	6.00	8.	494.00
4	120	215.00	4.30	6.00	720.00	505.00
5	128	263.00	6.00	6.00	768.00	505.00
6	132	312.00	12.25	6.00	792.00	480.00
7	122	360.00	–	6.00	732.00	9.

B. Interpreting Economic Data

Use the data from the production cost and revenue schedule to answer the questions.

10. How many centerpieces can the store produce before experiencing diminishing returns? Explain.

_____

_____

11. What happens to the store's profits from centerpieces when the manager adds a sixth worker? List some reasons why this might happen.

_____

_____

12. When has the store reached it's profit-maximizing potential? Explain. How many workers are employed?

_____

_____

13. At what point does the store experience negative returns? Explain.

_____

_____

Copyright © McDougal Littell/Houghton Mifflin Company.

CHAPTER 5

Name _____ Date _____

Classifying Economic Factors and Applying Economic Concepts

Six different factors cause changes in supply: input costs, labor productivity, technology, government actions, producer expectations, and number of producers. Read each of the situations below and decide which of the six factors it best illustrates. Write the characteristic, then tell what will happen to supply.

1. A software company invests in a set of fast, new computers that allow employees to test their new programs easily and quickly. Which factor is this and how will it affect supply?

_____

2. A farmer is deciding how much tobacco and how much corn to grow on the farm. Congress recently cut the subsidies that it pays farmers to raise tobacco. Which factor is this and how will it affect supply of both crops?

_____

3. A tool-making company hires several workers who got degrees from a technical school, where they learned manufacturing techniques. Which factor is this and how will it affect supply?

_____

4. A pancake restaurant is successful in a downtown mall. Another pancake restaurant opens up in a building across from the mall parking lot. Which factor is this and how will it change supply?

_____

5. You make a canned beverage for dieters that contains an extract from a plant. A law firm is bringing a lawsuit against another company that makes energy bars with this extract. They claim that the plant extract is harmful. Which factor is this and how will it change supply?

_____

6. You own a company that makes wire. The price of copper has recently gone up.

_____

7. You are a tea distributor. You have heard rumors that a new scientific study will soon announce that tea contains unique compounds that help prevent cancer. What factor is this and how will it change supply?

_____

Copyright © McDougal Littell/Houghton Mifflin Company.

CHAPTER 5

SECTION
4

RETEACHING ACTIVITY
What Is Elasticity of Supply?

A. Write "true" on the blank line if the statement is true. If the statement is false, write the corrected statement on the blank line.

EXAMPLES

The first president of the United States was <u>George Washington</u>. _true_____

The first president of the United States was <u>Abraham Lincoln</u>. _George Washington_____

1. Elasticity of supply is a measure of how responsive consumers are to changes in price.

_____

2. Supply is elastic if a 15 percent drop in price causes a decrease in quantity supplied greater than 15 percent.

_____

3. Supply is inelastic if a 15 percent drop in price causes an increase in quantity supplied that is greater than 15 percent.

_____

4. The supply curve of an item that has an elastic supply is steeper than the supply curve of an item that has an inelastic supply.

_____

5. Elasticity of supply for most products increases over time.

_____

B. Explaining Economic Concepts

Answer the questions in the space provided.

6. Name an item that has an inelastic supply. Explain why supply for this item tends to be inelastic.

_____

_____

7. The price of compact-fluorescent light bulbs drops from $4.00 to $2.50. The number of these light bulbs a supplier offers goes from 3,000 per month to 2,500 per month. Is this supply elastic or inelastic? Show your work in the space provided and explain your answer.

_____

_____

Copyright © McDougal Littell/Houghton Mifflin Company.

CHAPTER 5

SECTION
1 | RETEACHING ACTIVITY
Seeking Equilibrium: Supply and Demand

A. Applying Economic Concepts

Study the market demand and supply schedule. It gives economic information about promotional toothbrushes dentists can order to give their patients. Use the information from the market demand and supply schedule to create a market supply curve and a market demand curve for the promotional toothbrushes. Draw your curves on the grid below.

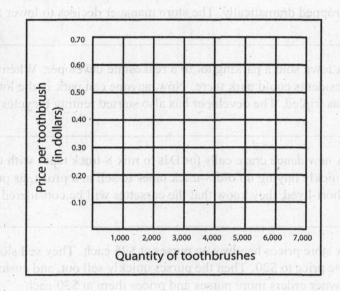

Price per Toothbrush (in dollars)	Quantity Supplied	Quantity Demanded
0.10	200	5,000
0.20	500	4,000
0.25	1,000	3,500
0.30	1,750	2,875
0.35	2,500	2,500
0.40	3,250	1,750
0.45	4,125	1,125
0.50	5,200	750
0.65	6,500	250

B. Analyzing and Interpreting Data

1. a. Circle the point of market equilibrium on the market supply and demand curves.

b. What is the equilibrium price?_____

2. If the producer decided to sell the toothbrushes for $0.40, would there be a shortage or a surplus of toothbrushes? Explain and tell how big the shortage or surplus would be.

_____

3. If the producer decided to sell the toothbrushes for $0.25, would there be a shortage or a surplus of toothbrushes? Explain and tell how big the shortage or surplus would be.

_____

4. a. Use arrows to show how a new technology that makes it easier and cheaper to print on plastic would change the market supply curve.

b. What would happen to the equilibrium price?_____

Copyright © McDougal Littell/Houghton Mifflin Company.

SECTION
2 | RETEACHING ACTIVITY
Prices as Signals and Incentives

A. Categorizing Situations Using Economic Concepts

The price system has four main characteristics: equality, independence, flexibility, and efficiency. Read each of the situations below and decide which of the four main characteristics of the price system it best illustrates. Write the characteristic on the line provided.

1. At a local toy store, a toy related to a children's movie sold well for several months after the movie was released. For the past month, the number of the toys the store has sold has dropped dramatically. The store manager decides to lower the price of the toy.

_____

2. A town sold a parking lot to a real estate developer. When the town ran the lot, only residents could park there. Now, anyone can park in the lot, and the price for parking has tripled. The developer has also started renting bicycles from a corner of the lot.

_____

3. A new dance craze calls for DJs to mix 8-track tapes with CDs. Many music stores are quickly buying up old 8-track tapes to sell at a profit, as prices rise. If the craze is short-lived, they know that the cassettes will be considered worthless again.

_____

4. A store prices handwoven purses at $25 each. They sell slowly, so the store owner drops the price to $20. Then the purses quickly sell out, and customers ask for more. The store owner orders more purses and prices them at $30 each.

_____

B. Explaining Economic Concepts

Write "true" on the blank line if the statement is true. If the statement is false, write the corrected statement on the blank line.

5. A rise in the price of a product signals to consumers it is a good time to buy the product.

_____

6. A shortage signals to producers that it is a good time to enter a market.

_____

7. Producers often lower prices as an incentive to consumers when a shortage occurs.

_____

Copyright © McDougal Littell/Houghton Mifflin Company.

SECTION 3 RETEACHING ACTIVITY

Intervention in the Price System

A. Reviewing Economic Vocabulary

Select the terms that best complete the sentences. Write the terms in the blanks. You will use some terms more than once.

black market	minimum wage	price ceiling
price floor	rationing	

1. During times of war, a government might use _____ to help distribute scarce resources.
2. To ensure that producers receive at least a certain amount for a particular good or service, a government might set a _____ , which is the minimum price a buyer must pay for the good or service.
3. People establish a _____ to exchange goods and services, skirting rules related to price interventions.
4. Federal law and some state laws have set a _____, which is the lowest price an employer can pay a worker for an hour of labor.
5. To ensure that consumers with lower incomes are not excluded from buying a particular good or service, the government might set a _____, which is the maximum price a seller may charge for the good or service.
6. The _____ is an example of a _____.

B. Comparing and Contrasting Economic Concepts

Fill in the table to describe the differences between price floors and price ceilings.

	Price Floor	Price Ceiling
In relation to equilibrium price		
Results in a . . .		
Fun fictional example stated as a news headline		

Copyright © McDougal Littell/Houghton Mifflin Company.

CHAPTER 7

Copyright © McDougal Littell/Houghton Mifflin Company.

SECTION 1 | RETEACHING ACTIVITY
What Is Perfect Competition?

A. Finding Main Ideas

Complete each sentence with the most appropriate term.

market structure	price taker
perfect competition	imperfect competition
standardized product	

1. A _____ has different producers but seems identical to consumers.

2. When the price of a product is determined by supply and demand, the maker of the product becomes a _____.

3. _____ occurs in markets having few sellers.

4. Economists use _____ to examine competition.

5. The ideal model of a market economy is _____.

B. Making Inferences

The following provides information about an annual craft fair. Use the information as the basis for your answers to the questions that follow.

200 sellers	Wide range of products
1,500 buyers	$50 booth fee per seller

6. Are the buyers and sellers at the craft fair likely to be independent and well-informed? Explain your answer.

_____

_____

7. Which additional characteristic or characteristics of the craft fair come close to perfect competition?

_____

_____

8. Name one or more characteristics of perfect competition that the craft fair is lacking.

_____

_____

SECTION 2 | RETEACHING ACTIVITY
The Impact of Monopoly

Explaining Economic Concepts

Write the letter of the term before the definition that best describes it.

a. monopoly
b. cartel
c. price maker
d. barrier to entry
e. natural monopoly
f. government monopoly
g. technological monopoly
h. geographic monopoly
i. economies of scale
j. patent

_____ **1.** exclusive right to a process or invention

_____ **2.** keeps new business from entering a market

_____ **3.** business that controls a manufacturing method or invention

_____ **4.** situation that occurs when production costs fall as producer grows

_____ **5.** business that is run or authorized by the government

_____ **6.** least competitive market structure

_____ **7.** business that can set prices without concern over competitors

_____ **8.** business that exists when lowest production costs occur with only one producer

_____ **9.** organization of sellers and producers who work to set prices and limit output

_____ **10.** business without nearby competitors

Copyright © McDougal Littell/Houghton Mifflin Company.

CHAPTER 7

SECTION
3 | RETEACHING ACTIVITY
Other Market Structures

Comparing and Contrasting Economic Information Write "true" on the blank line if the statement is true. If the statement is false, write the corrected statement on the blank line.

1. Monopolistic competition involves many buyers and sellers. _____

_____

2. An oligopoly has few buyers and sellers. _____

_____

3. Standardized products are characteristic of monopolistic competition. _____

_____

4. Differentiated products are characteristic of monopolistic competition but not of monopolies. _____

_____

5. Very few manufacturing industries in the United States are oligopolistic. _____

_____

6. Competitors in monopolistic markets use nonprice competition. _____

_____

7. Sellers in an oligopoly have more control over prices than sellers in monopolistic competition. _____

_____

8. Start-up costs to enter a market ruled by monopolistic competition are about the same as start-up costs to enter an oligopolistic market. _____

_____

Copyright © McDougal Littell/Houghton Mifflin Company.

SECTION
4 | RETEACHING ACTIVITY
Regulation and Deregulation Today

Generalizing from Economic Information

A. The following questions deal with government regulation of business. Answer them in the space provided.

1. Why did the U.S. government become concerned about trusts?

_____

_____

_____

2. What power do antitrust laws give to the government?

_____

_____

_____

3. What is the responsibility of the Federal Trade Commission?

_____

_____

_____

4. Under what circumstances does the government issue cease and desist orders?

_____

_____

_____

5. Why does the government enforce a policy of public disclosure?

_____

_____

_____

B. Write a general statement about government regulation. Use the answers you gave as a basis for your statement.

Copyright © McDougal Littell/Houghton Mifflin Company.

SECTION 1 | RETEACHING ACTIVITY
Sole Proprietorships

Explaining Economic Concepts

The following questions deal with sole proprietorships. Answer them in the space provided.

1. What is a sole proprietorship?

_____

_____

2. How do sole proprietorships earn a profit?

_____

_____

3. What does setting up a sole proprietorship involve?

_____

_____

_____

4. What are the advantages of a sole proprietorship?

_____

_____

_____

5. How might unlimited liability affect a sole proprietor if the business fails?

_____

_____

6. What are the other limitations of a sole proprietorship?

_____

_____

_____

Copyright © McDougal Littell/Houghton Mifflin Company.

CHAPTER 8

SECTION
2 | RETEACHING ACTIVITY
Forms of Partnerships

Conducting Marginal Cost-Marginal Benefit Analysis

Read the situation and the list of considerations. Then use the information to make a marginal cost-marginal benefit analysis. Complete the chart to help you do so. Base the decision on how you assess the added costs and benefits.

Situation: A sole proprietor is deciding whether or not to form a partnership with a close friend. She has already completed a cost-benefit analysis and believes that the partnership will be financially profitable. However, there are added costs and benefits to be considered.

Considerations

Limited life   Unlimited liability
Easy set-up   Easy to dissolve
Greater resources   Few government regulations
Potential for disagreements   Possibility of straining the friendship
Possibility of specializing

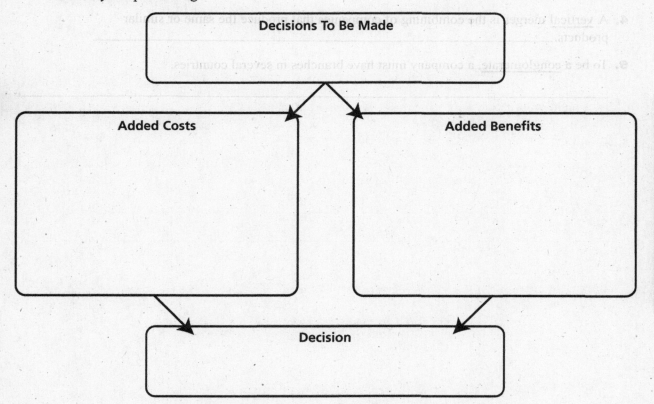

Decisions To Be Made

Added Costs   **Added Benefits**

Decision

1. Explain why you made the decision you did.

_____

_____

_____

Copyright © McDougal Littell/Houghton Mifflin Company.

CHAPTER 8

SECTION 3 | RETEACHING ACTIVITY
Corporations, Mergers, and Multinationals

Comparing and Contrasting Economic Information Write *true* in the blank if the statement is true. If the statement is false, make it correct by writing a replacement for the underlined word(s). See the examples provided below.

EXAMPLES

The first president of the United States was <u>George Washington</u>. *true*

The first president of the United States was <u>Abraham Lincoln</u>. *George Washington*

1. Corporations may issue both <u>stocks and bonds</u>. _____

2. Corporate <u>bonds</u> pay dividends. _____

3. <u>Both public and private</u> companies issue stock. _____

4. A <u>vertical</u> merger is the combining of companies that produce the same or similar products. _____

5. To be a <u>conglomerate</u>, a company must have branches in several countries.

_____

Copyright © McDougal Littell/Houghton Mifflin Company.

CHAPTER 8

Name
Date

Copyright © McDougal Littell/Houghton Mifflin Company.

SECTION 4 | RETEACHING ACTIVITY
Franchises, Co-ops, and Nonprofits

A. Making Inferences

Below are some general statements about three types of business organizations. Read each statement. Then supply details from the section to support it.

1. A franchise is made up of semi-independent businesses.

   a. _____

   b. _____

2. A franchise offers several "built-in" benefits.

   a. _____

   b. _____

3. Franchises also have disadvantages.

   a. _____

   b. _____

4. Cooperatives operate for the shared benefit of their owners.

   a. _____

   b. _____

5. Nonprofit businesses are organized for reasons other than making a profit.

   a. _____

   b. _____

6. The structure of a nonprofit resembles that of a corporation.

   a. _____

   b. _____

CHAPTER 8

Name _____ Date _____

How Are Wages Determined?

Analyzing Cause and Effect

The following is a chart showing causes and their effects on wage rates. Complete the chart by filling in the cause or effect.

Cause   Effect

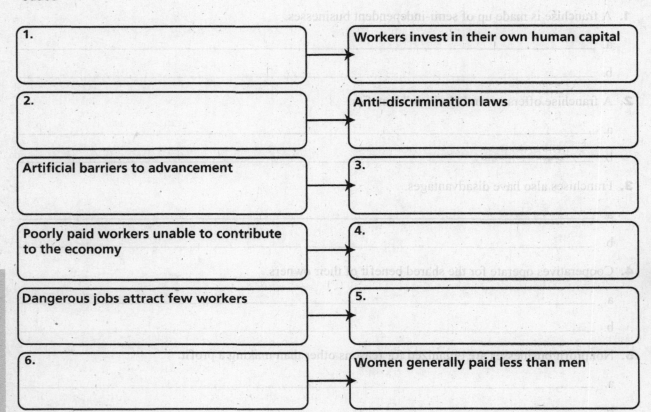

Cause	Effect
1.	Workers invest in their own human capital
2.	Anti–discrimination laws
Artificial barriers to advancement	3.
Poorly paid workers unable to contribute to the economy	4.
Dangerous jobs attract few workers	5.
6.	Women generally paid less than men

Copyright © McDougal Littell/Houghton Mifflin Company.

CHAPTER 9

Copyright © McDougal Littell/Houghton Mifflin Company.

SECTION
2 | RETEACHING ACTIVITY
Trends in Today's Labor Market

A. Making Inferences

Below are some general statements about the current labor market. Read each statement. Then supply details from the section to support it.

1. Women have added to the growth of the labor market.

a. _____

b. _____

2. U.S. workers are well educated.

a. _____

b. _____

3. Today's labor market is global.

a. _____

b. _____

4. Service-related jobs make up the largest economic sector in the United States.

a. _____

b. _____

5. Technology has changed the way people work.

a. _____

b. _____

6. Businesses are hiring more part-time workers.

a. _____

b. _____

CHAPTER 9

CHAPTER 9

SECTION
3 | RETEACHING ACTIVITY
Organized Labor in the United States

A. Drawing Conclusions

Complete the diagram by writing a conclusion about the current strength of organized labor in the United States. Support your conclusion with three facts about labor unions.

Fact	Fact	Fact

Conclusion

B. Clarifying

Write the term next to its definition.

craft union   union shop
industrial union   collective bargaining
closed shop   binding arbitration

7. Negotiations between businesses and their
   employees: _____

8. A business where workers must join a union
   within a certain period of time: _____

9. An organization of workers with different
   skills who work in the same industry: _____

10. A business where an employer must hire only
    union members: _____

11. An organization of workers with similar skills
    who work in different industries: _____

Copyright © McDougal Littell/Houghton Mifflin Company.

SECTION 1 | RETEACHING ACTIVITY
Money: Its Functions and Properties

A. Explaining Economic Concepts
Complete each sentence with the most appropriate term.

medium of exchange	representative money
barter	fiat money
standard of value	currency
store of value	demand deposits
commodity money	near money

1. Trading repair work at an apartment building for a free apartment is an example of

   _____

2. When money measures what something is worth, it functions as a

   _____

3. Because they have value, gold, silver, and salt have all been used as

   _____

4. _____ is defined as paper money and coins.

5. When the dollar was taken off the gold standard it became _____.

6. Checking accounts are also called _____.

7. Precious metals are used to back up _____.

8. Forms of _____ include savings accounts and time deposits.

9. During periods of inflation, money does not function well as a

   _____

10. A _____ is the means through which goods and services can be

    exchanged.

Copyright © McDougal Littell/Houghton Mifflin Company.

CHAPTER 10

SECTION
2

RETEACHING ACTIVITY

The Development of U.S. Banking

A. Making Inferences

The following questions deal with the development of banking in the United States. Answer them in the space provided.

1. Did state chartering of banks in early America make deposits secure? Give reasons to support your answer.

_____

_____

2. How did Hamilton's belief in a strong central government lead to the creation of a national bank?

_____

_____

3. How did opposition to the First Bank of the United States contribute to economic instability?

_____

_____

4. Did President Jackson's mistrust of banks affect the nation's economy? Explain your answer.

_____

_____

5. What did President Franklin Roosevelt hope to accomplish by increasing government regulation of banking?

_____

_____

6. How did deregulation contribute to economic instability?

_____

_____

Copyright © McDougal Littell/Houghton Mifflin Company.

CHAPTER 10

SECTION
3 | RETEACHING ACTIVITY
Innovations in Modern Banking

Analyzing Cause and Effect

Complete the chart below by writing the effects of each cause.

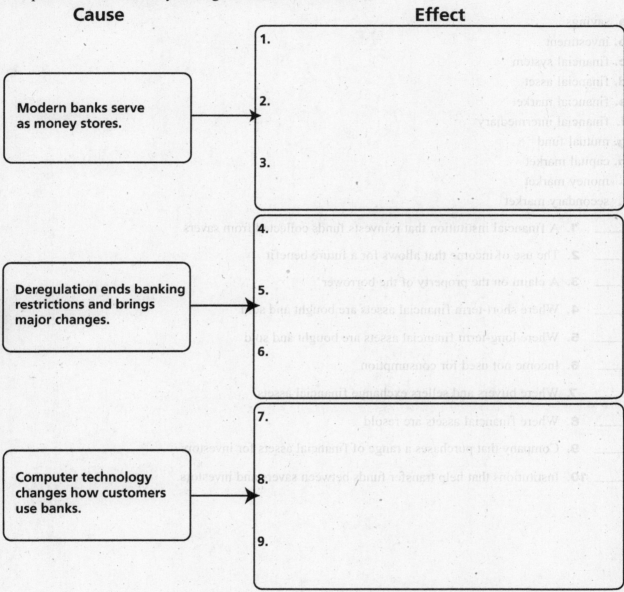

Cause   **Effect**

| Modern banks serve as money stores. | 1. 2. 3. |

| Deregulation ends banking restrictions and brings major changes. | 4. 5. 6. |

| Computer technology changes how customers use banks. | 7. 8. 9. |

Copyright © McDougal Littell/Houghton Mifflin Company.

CHAPTER 10

CHAPTER 11

SECTION
1

RETEACHING ACTIVITY
Savings and Investments

Explaining Economic Concepts

Write the letter of the term before the description that best explains it.

a. savings
b. investment
c. financial system
d. financial asset
e. financial market
f. financial intermediary
g. mutual fund
h. capital market
i. money market
j. secondary market

_____ **1.** A financial institution that reinvests funds collected from savers

_____ **2.** The use of income that allows for a future benefit

_____ **3.** A claim on the property of the borrower

_____ **4.** Where short-term financial assets are bought and sold

_____ **5.** Where long-term financial assets are bought and sold

_____ **6.** Income not used for consumption

_____ **7.** Where buyers and sellers exchange financial assets

_____ **8.** Where financial assets are resold

_____ **9.** Company that purchases a range of financial assets for investors

_____ **10.** Institutions that help transfer funds between savers and investors

Copyright © McDougal Littell/Houghton Mifflin Company.

SECTION 2 | RETEACHING ACTIVITY
Investing in a Market Economy

A. Applying Economic Concepts The following are statements about investing. If the statement is true, write *true* in the blank . If the statement is false, write the correct statement on the line provided. See the examples given below.

EXAMPLES

The first president of the United States was <u>George Washington</u>.   *true* _____

The first president of the United States was <u>Abraham Lincoln</u>.   *George Washington* _____

---

1. Deciding on a <u>financial goal</u> is the first step in making an investment.

_____

2. The amount of money available after meeting all current expenses is an <u>income</u> issue for investors.

_____

3. Debts are an investment issue, since <u>income</u> on debt is not likely to be higher than investment earnings.

_____

4. <u>Long-term</u> investments are called for when saving for emergencies.

_____

5. Timing is an issue when investing in <u>CDs</u>.

_____

6. The purpose of <u>liquidity</u> is to purchase stock from more than one corporation.

_____

7. Purchasing stock carries <u>less</u> risk than investing in CDs.

_____

8. In general, investments that involve greater risk are likely to yield <u>higher</u> returns.

_____

Copyright © McDougal Littell/Houghton Mifflin Company.

CHAPTER 11

SECTION 3 | RETEACHING ACTIVITY
Buying and Selling Stocks

A. Comparing and Contrasting Economic Information

The two graphs show stock performances from May 2005 through June 2006 on two indexes. Use the information shown by the graphs and your knowledge of stock markets to answer the questions below.

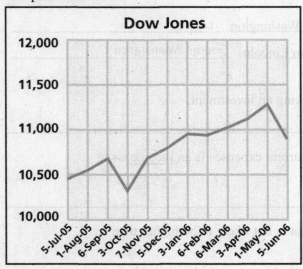

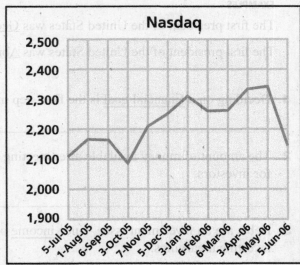

1. When did each index reach its peak?

_____

2. When did each index reach its lowest point?

_____

3. In general, how do the performances of the two indexes compare?

_____

4. What is the most common characteristic of the stocks included on the Dow? on the NASDAQ?

_____

5. What type of trading does the NASDAQ accommodate? How?

_____

Copyright © McDougal Littell/Houghton Mifflin Company.

CHAPTER 11

SECTION
4

RETEACHING ACTIVITY
Bonds and Other Financial Instruments

A. Analyzing Economic Data

This graph shows the yields of industrial corporate bonds at different maturity dates. One curve represents bonds rated AAA, the other curve is for bonds rated BBB. Use the graph and your knowledge of bonds to answer the questions.

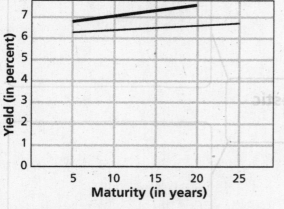

1. Which type of bond has the higher yield?

_____

2. Approximately what is the difference in the yield of BBB-rated bonds that mature in 5 years and in 15 years?

_____

3. Approximately how much did the yield of AAA-rated bonds with different maturity rates vary?

_____

4. Which type of bond bears the greater risk? Explain your answer.

_____

5. Would an investor wishing to make a long-term investment be more likely to purchase bonds rated AAA or BBB? Why?

_____

6. Compare the two yield curves. How are they the same? How are they different?

_____

Copyright © McDougal Littell/Houghton Mifflin Company.

CHAPTER 11

CHAPTER 12

SECTION **1** | RETEACHING ACTIVITY
Gross Domestic Product and Other Indicators

A. Explaining Economic Concepts

Complete the diagram by adding the four economic sectors used to calculate GDP.

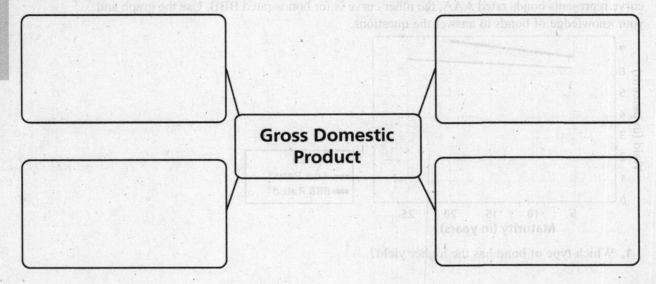

B. Explaining Economic Concepts

Complete each sentence with the appropriate term.

real GDP	gross national product (GNP)
nonmarket activities	net national product (NNP)
underground economy	national income (NI)

1. _____ is corrected for changes in prices from year to year.

2. GDP does not measure the _____ nor _____.

3. The market value of all final goods and services produced by a country is

_____.

4. The value of final goods and services less the value of worn-out capital goods is

_____.

5. To calculate _____, economists subtract indirect business taxes

from NNP.

Copyright © McDougal Littell/Houghton Mifflin Company.

SECTION
2 | RETEACHING ACTIVITY
Business Cycles

A. Explaining Economic Concepts

Select the letter of the term, name, or phrase that best matches each description.

a. business cycle
b. economic growth
c. recession
d. stagflation
e. aggregate demand
f. aggregate supply
g. macroeconomic equilibrium
h. leading indicators
i. coincident indicators
j. lagging indicators

_____ **1.** total amount of goods and services that producers will provide at each and every price level

_____ **2.** economic contraction lasting at least two quarters

_____ **3.** increase in a nation's real GDP

_____ **4.** period of rising prices and slowing business activity

_____ **5.** measures of economic performance that usually change before real GDP changes

_____ **6.** point at which aggregate demand equals aggregate supply

_____ **7.** series of growing and shrinking periods of economic activity

_____ **8.** extended period of high unemployment and reduced business activity

_____ **9.** measures of economic performance that usually change at the same time as real GDP changes

_____ **10.** total amount of goods and services that households, businesses, government, and foreign purchasers will buy at each and every price level

Copyright © McDougal Littell/Houghton Mifflin Company.

CHAPTER 12

SECTION
3

RETEACHING ACTIVITY
Stimulating Economic Growth

Making Inferences

Complete the chart below by identifying four factors that change productivity. Then write
what you can infer about how the factor affects productivity.

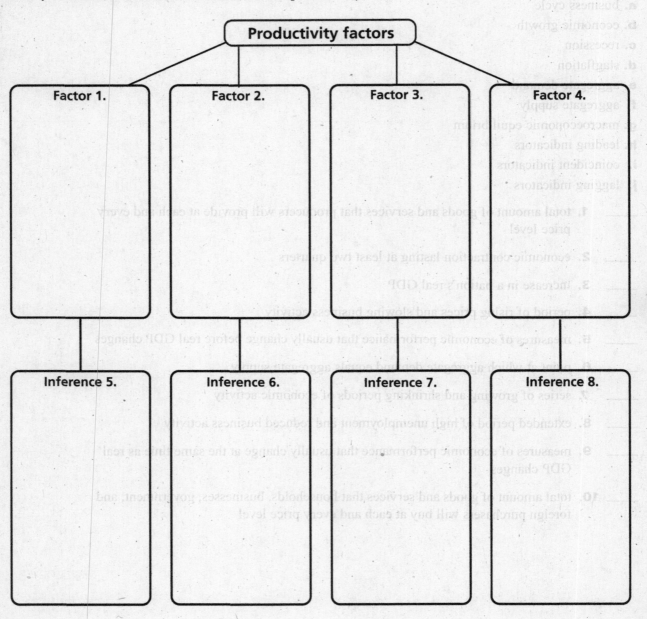

Copyright © McDougal Littell/Houghton Mifflin Company.

Economics: Concepts and Choices
Chapter 12: Economic Indicators and Measurements

SECTION 1 | RETEACHING ACTIVITY
Unemployment in Today's Economy

A. Classifying Types of Unemployment

There are four different types of unemployment: frictional, seasonal, structural, and cyclical. Read each of the situations below, and decide which category of unemployment it describes. Write the category on the line provided.

1. When a company outsources work to a firm in Malaysia, 25 customer service representatives lose their jobs. To get similar-paying jobs in their area, they need extensive training.

   _____

2. A sister and brother close the rug-cleaning business they ran together for three years. The brother wants to become a chef and is looking for work as a chef's assistant. The sister has trained as a translator for deaf people and is looking for such work.

   _____

3. A family-owned publishing company in a small town is looking for a managing editor to help expand their new children's book department. Although many people in the region are looking for work, the company cannot find a qualified person for the position.

   _____

4. For the past couple of months, you have been working as an arts and crafts teacher at a local day camp. Your job will end soon, and you are looking for another full-time job.

   _____

5. You have served for four years in the army. You are looking for a civilian job running a warehouse, which is similar to the job you did for the past two years in the military.

   _____

B. Explaining Economic Concepts

Answer the following questions about unemployment and the economy.

6. How does an underemployed worker differ from an unemployed worker?

   _____

   _____

7. During a period of full employment, the nation still has an unemployment rate of 4 percent. Why is there still unemployment during periods of full employment, and what is the main type of unemployment that occurs at those times?

   _____

   _____

Copyright © McDougal Littell/Houghton Mifflin Company.

SECTION
2 | RETEACHING ACTIVITY
Poverty and Income Distribution

A. Reviewing Economic Vocabulary

Match the numbered definition with the term that best defines it. Write the letter of your answer in the blank.

a. income distribution
b. income inequality
c. poverty
d. poverty rate

e. poverty threshold
f. welfare
g. workfare

_____ 1. the official minimum income needed for the bare necessities of life in the U.S.

_____ 2. the way income is divided among the nation's people

_____ 3. the condition of living beneath a minimum standard

_____ 4. government-run programs that assist people with low incomes

_____ 5. the disproportionate division of income

_____ 6. a program that requires welfare recipients to work

_____ 7. the percentage of people in households living below a minimum standard

B. Describing Causes of Poverty

Answer the questions about the factors and causes of poverty.

8. Why has a rise in the birthrate among unmarried women and in the divorce rate led to an increase in poverty?

9. How does discrimination affect poverty?

10. How have labor force changes affected poverty?

Copyright © McDougal Littell/Houghton Mifflin Company.

SECTION
3

RETEACHING ACTIVITY

Causes and Consequences of Inflation

A. Reviewing Economic Vocabulary

Select the term that best completes each sentence. Write the letter of the term in the blank.

a. consumer price index   **e.** demand-pull inflation   **i.** moderate inflation
b. cost-push inflation   **f.** galloping inflation   **j.** negligible inflation
c. creeping inflation   **g.** hyperinflation   **k.** producer price index
d. deflation   **h.** inflation

_____ **1.** A sustained rise in prices for a variety of goods and services is called

_____ **2.** A sustained rise in prices caused by a sharp rise in the cost of resources or labor is known as

_____ **3.** A sustained drop in prices of a variety of goods and services is called

_____ **4.** An inflation rate of between 1 percent and 3 percent per year is considered to be

_____ **5.** Economists commonly measure the changes in wholesale prices by compiling the

_____ **6.** An inflation rate of more than 500 percent per year is called

_____ **7.** An inflation rate of less than 1 percent per year is considered to be

_____ **8.** Economists measure the changes in prices of goods and services the general public commonly purchased by compiling the

_____ **9.** If the inflation rate rises rapidly over a short period of time, but the rate stays below 500 percent per year, economists say that there is

_____ **10.** A sustained rise in prices caused by rising consumers purchases when the goods and services are in short supply is called

_____ **11.** If the inflation rate remains at 1 percent to 3 percent per year over the course of many years, economists say there is

Copyright © McDougal Littell/Houghton Mifflin Company.

SECTION 1 | RETEACHING ACTIVITY
How Taxes Work

A. Classifying Principles of and Criteria for Taxation

There are two principles of taxation: benefit-received and ability-to-pay. There are three criteria for taxation: equity, simplicity, and efficiency. Read each of the tax descriptions below and decide which principle and/or which criterion it best illustrates. Write the principle, the criterion, or both on the lines.

1. _____ A state charges a fee for a fishing license for everyone over the age of 17 who wants to fish.

2. _____ Sporting stores sell the licenses and send the money to the state each month.

3. _____ A local government considers lowering the tax rate for people on the city payroll and raising the tax rate for everyone else. But it decides the plan would violate a basic criteria of taxation.

4. _____ The federal government sets up a tax that has higher rates for people who have large incomes and lower rates for people who have lower incomes. People whose incomes are close to, at, or below the poverty threshold pay no income tax.

5. _____ The government collects the income tax through payroll deductions.

B. Explaining Economic Concepts

Write T in the blank if the statement is true. If the statement is false, write F in the blank and then write the corrected statement on the line below.

6. _____ With a progressive tax, the tax rate is the same for all taxpayers. _____
_____

7. _____ A sales tax on food is a regressive tax. _____
_____

8. _____ The government decides to tax homeowners' electricity usage; the incidence of the tax is most likely to fall on the consumer rather than the producer. _____
_____

Copyright © McDougal Littell/Houghton Mifflin Company.

SECTION
2 | RETEACHING ACTIVITY
Federal Taxes

A. Reviewing Different Kinds of Federal Taxes

Fill in the chart to review information about the main types of federal taxes.

Type of tax	Description	Tax structure	Who pays	Tax rate	Percent of federal revenue it raises
Individual income tax					
Social Security tax					
Medicare tax					
Unemployment tax				x	
Corporate income tax					
Estate tax		x	x	x	
Gift tax		x	x	x	
Excise tax		x	x	x	
Customs duties		x	x	x	
User fees		x		x	

Copyright © McDougal Littell/Houghton Mifflin Company.

CHAPTER 14

SECTION
3

RETEACHING ACTIVITY
Federal Government Spending

A. Reviewing Economics Vocabulary

Select the term or terms that best complete each incomplete sentence. Write the terms in the blanks.

allocations	discretionary spending	entitlement	federal budget
grant-in-aid		Medicaid	Medicare
redistribution of income	mandatory spending	Social Security	
	resource allocation		

The federal government has two different kinds of expenditures.

_____ is spending for programs that the federal government

must authorize each year. Spending for education, natural resource protection,

science research, federal courts, and the military all undergo yearly review for their

_____. _____ is spending that is required

by current law. The following _____ programs legally must be

fully funded every year: _____, _____, and

_____. Other programs in this category include Food Stamps,

unemployment insurance, homeland security, and border defense. Congress and the president

work together on the _____. Both have offices that give guidelines for

realistic estimates of how much money different programs and agencies need to run well. The

federal government spends money directly on goods and services it uses. It makes transfer

payments for programs that help people with low incomes and the elderly. It also makes

transfer payments to state and local governments for specific programs, such as highway

construction. Such payments are called _____ payments. By spending

trillions of dollars every year, the federal government has a large affect on the economy. It

influences _____ by choosing goods and services to buy and by selecting

specific types of programs to fund. It affects household incomes through taxation and direct

payment to families with low incomes. In this way, the federal government influences the

_____.

Copyright © McDougal Littell/Houghton Mifflin Company.

SECTION
4 | RETEACHING ACTIVITY
State and Local Taxes and Spending

A. Analyzing Economic Information

Refer to the graphs on page 437 of *Economics: Concepts and Choices*. Use the spaces provided to answer the following questions about these graphs.

1. Which level of government gets 0.3% of its revenue from corporate income tax? What percentage of revenue does the other level of government get from this tax?

_____

2. What are the two largest sources of revenue for both state and local governments?

_____

3. Which source provides one-quarter of the revenue for local government but only 1% of the revenue for state government?

_____

4. Which level of government gets a greater percentage of its revenue from sales tax?

_____

B. Determining Which Level of Government Is Most Likely to Make an Expenditure

Read each of the descriptions below and decide which whether a state government or a local government is most likely to make the expenditure. Write your answer in the space provided.

5. _____Over the course of the winter, a series of large potholes forms in a county road. Which level of government is most likely to spend the money to repair this road?

6. _____A crime lab decides to invest in a set of equipment and chemicals that will make it very easy to do DNA testing of materials from a crime scene. Which level of government is most likely to pay for the equipment and chemicals?

7. _____An elderly couple with a low income has large medical bills from testing at a local hospital. Which level of government is most likely to pay the couple's medical expenses?

8. _____Three towns, each with a large Finnish population, decide to put on a cultural festival. Which level of government is most likely to pay for the festival?

9. _____The blinking light in an overhead traffic signal burns out. Which level of government is most likely to spend the money to fix the light?

Copyright © McDougal Littell/Houghton Mifflin Company.

CHAPTER 14

CHAPTER 15

**SECTION
1** | RETEACHING ACTIVITY
What Is Fiscal Policy?

A. Categorizing Fiscal Policy Tools

There are two types of fiscal policy tools. The first are *automatic stabilizers*, which include *public transfer payments* and *progressive income taxes*. The second is *discretionary fiscal policy*, which is either *expansionary* or *contractionary*. Read each of the situations below and decide which type of tool is described and which example of the tool is being employed. Write your answers on the lines.

1. One of two wage-earners in a family becomes unemployed for several months. The family's income drops and they move into a lower tax bracket that year.

   Fiscal tool_____ Type or feature of policy_____

2. The Department of Agriculture cuts funding for a program to hold free seminars on beekeeping.

   Fiscal tool_____ Type or feature of policy_____

3. Congress introduces and passes a bill to exempt households at or below the poverty threshold from paying individual income taxes. The president signs the bill into law.

   Fiscal tool_____ Type or feature of policy_____

4. An unemployed accountant finds a new job; his family no longer qualifies for food stamps.

   Fiscal tool_____ Type or feature of policy_____

5. The public schools in twenty large cities receive funding to provide free lunches to students from low-income households throughout the summer.

   Fiscal tool_____ Type or feature of policy_____

6. The president signs a bill into law that requires all corporations selling goods in the United States to pay a flat tax rate on the profits they make on those sales.

   Fiscal tool_____ Type or feature of policy_____

7. Congress overrides a presidential veto on a bill cutting Medicaid benefits payments to people in households earning more than two-thirds the poverty threshold.

   Fiscal tool_____ Type or feature of policy_____

Copyright © McDougal Littell/Houghton Mifflin Company.

Copyright © McDougal Littell/Houghton Mifflin Company.

SECTION 2 | RETEACHING ACTIVITY
Demand-Side and Supply-Side Policies

A. Distinguishing Fact from Opinion

For each of the statements below, decide whether it is a fact or an opinion. Write F in the blank if the statement is a fact; then write an opinion related to the fact on the line below. Write O in the blank if the statement is an opinion; then write a fact related to the opinion on the line below.

1. _____ The government should have a limited role in the nation's economy.

   _____

2. _____ Arthur Laffer suggested that a high tax rate reduces government revenues by discouraging people from working hard.

   _____

3. _____ Based on the multiplier effect, a small decrease in business investment can cause a large decrease in economic activity.

   _____

4. _____ During times of recession, the government needs to spend money on public programs to help stimulate aggregate demand.

   _____

5. _____ Cutting government regulation is the best way to get businesses to increase production and to spur general economic growth.

   _____

6. _____ John Keynes formulated demand-side fiscal policies in the early years of the Great Depression.

   _____

7. _____ Governments often have difficulty cutting popular programs meant to spur the economy once the economy has recovered.

   _____

B. Designing a Poster

On the back of this paper or on a separate sheet of paper, create a poster to promote either demand-side or supply-side economics. Your poster should have a strong central image, a slogan, and an explanation or fact supporting your slogan.

SECTION
3 | RETEACHING ACTIVITY
Deficits and the National Debt

CHAPTER 15

A. Reviewing Economic Vocabulary

Select the term that best completes each sentence. Write the term in the blank.

balanced budget
budget deficit
budget surplus
deficit spending
national debt

1. When the government makes a practice of spending more than it collects in revenue in each of many budget years, we say that the government is engaging in _____.
2. The government runs a _____ when it collects more in revenue than it spends in a given budget year.
3. When the government collects the same amount in revenue as it spends in a particular budget year, the government has a _____.
4. The government runs a _____ when it spends more than it collects in revenue in a given budget year.
5. The total amount of money that the government owes is called _____.

B. Analyzing Causes and Effects

Fill in the charts to analyze causes of deficit spending and effects of a large national debt.

Causes of Deficit Spending
6.
7.
8.
9.

Effects of Long-term National Debt
10.
11.
12.

Copyright © McDougal Littell/Houghton Mifflin Company.

SECTION
1 | RETEACHING ACTIVITY
The Federal Reserve System

A. Explaining Economic Concepts

The following questions deal with the Federal Reserve System. Answer them in the space provided.

1. Why did Congress create the Federal Reserve System?

_____

_____

2. How does the Fed supervise banking in the United States?

_____

_____

3. Why is the Fed important in times of emergency?

_____

_____

4. What is the relationship between the Fed and the federal government?

_____

_____

_____

5. Why is the Fed considered to be a "banker's bank"?

_____

_____

_____

6. What type of structure does the Fed have?

_____

_____

7. What role does the Board of Governors play?

_____

_____

_____

8. How do financial institutions become members of the Federal Reserve System?

_____

_____

_____

Copyright © McDougal Littell/Houghton Mifflin Company.

CHAPTER 16

CHAPTER 16

SECTION 2 | RETEACHING ACTIVITY
Functions of the Federal Reserve

A. Applying Economic Concepts

The following questions deal with services that the Federal Reserve System provides. Write your answers in the spaces provided.

1. A bank is located in a town that depends heavily on winter tourism. How might the Fed be called upon to assist that bank in the summer? Explain.

   _____

   _____

2. Joan receives a check every week in the summer from the coffee shop where she works part-time. What role does the Fed play in enabling her employer to pay with a check?

   _____

   _____

3. When Jason was born, his parents opened an account at a local bank to save money for his college tuition. Explain one way the Fed safeguards that money until Jason needs it.

   _____

   _____

4. Explain how the Fed is acting as the government's banker when it issues a Social Security check.

   _____

   _____

5. When the Fed raises the required reserve ratio, how does this affect a commercial bank's ability to create money? Explain your answer.

   _____

   _____

6. Why is the Fed concerned with income levels?

   _____

   _____

Copyright © McDougal Littell/Houghton Mifflin Company.

SECTION
3 | RETEACHING ACTIVITY
Monetary Policy

A. Explaining Economic Concepts

Write the letter of each term on the line before the definition that best describes it.

a. monetary policy
b. discount rate
c. prime rate
d. open market operations
e. federal funds rate
f. expansionary monetary policy
g. easy-money policy
h. contractionary monetary policy
i. tight-money policy
j. monetarism

_____ **1.** Another term for contractionary monetary policy

_____ **2.** The purchase and sale of bonds

_____ **3.** What banks pay when borrowing from one another

_____ **4.** What the Fed charges when lending to other banks

_____ **5.** Includes any action of the Fed that changes the money supply

_____ **6.** A plan to increase the money supply

_____ **7.** Theory stating that rapid changes in the money supply cause economic instability

_____ **8.** Another name for expansionary money supply

_____ **9.** A plan to decrease the money supply

_____ **10.** What banks charge their best customers

Copyright © McDougal Littell/Houghton Mifflin Company.

CHAPTER 16

CHAPTER 16

SECTION
4 | RETEACHING ACTIVITY
Applying Monetary and Fiscal Policy

A. Analyzing Cause and Effect

The following questions deal with fiscal and monetary policies. Write your answers in the spaces provided.

1. When is the government most likely to offer tax cuts? Why?

_____

_____

2. How does the Fed use open market operations to affect the economy?

_____

_____

3. What is most likely to happen when the timing of an economic policy is poor?

_____

_____

4. Why does the Fed raise the discount rate? When is it most likely to do so?

_____

_____

5. What is the effect on real GDP of expansionary policies? Of contractionary policies?

_____

_____

6. Is the coordination of economic policies important? Explain.

_____

_____

Copyright © McDougal Littell/Houghton Mifflin Company.

SECTION
1

RETEACHING ACTIVITY

Benefits and Issues of International Trade

A. Finding Main Ideas

The following questions deal with international trade. Answer them in the space provided.

1. Is specialization to a nation's economic advantage?

_____

_____

2. How does specialization increase economic interdependence?

_____

_____

3. When does a nation have an absolute advantage over another?

_____

_____

4. When does a nation have a comparative advantage over another?

_____

_____

5. How do countries benefit from free trade?

_____

_____

6. What effect do exports have on prices and quantity?

_____

_____

7. How can domestic producers benefit from imports?

_____

_____

8. How does trade affect employment?

_____

_____

Copyright © McDougal Littell/Houghton Mifflin Company.

CHAPTER 17

SECTION
2 | RETEACHING ACTIVITY
Trade Barriers

A. Explaining Economic Concepts

Write the letter of the term on the line before the definition that matches it.

a. tariff

b. trade barrier

c. embargo

d. protective tariffs

e. dumping

f. revenue tariffs

g. trade war

h. protectionism

i. quota

j. infant industries

k. voluntary export restraint

_____ **1.** Law that limits free trade

_____ **2.** Limit on the amount of a product that can be imported

_____ **3.** Fee charged for imported goods

_____ **4.** Country's self-imposed limit on exports

_____ **5.** Law that cuts off most or all trade with another country

_____ **6.** Sale of a product in another country at a price lower than that charged in the home market

_____ **7.** Taxes on imports to raise money

_____ **8.** Taxes on imports to protect domestic goods

_____ **9.** Series of increasing trade barriers between nations

_____ **10.** Use of trade barriers to protect domestic industries

CHAPTER 17

Copyright © McDougal Littell/Houghton Mifflin Company.

Copyright © McDougal Littell/Houghton Mifflin Company.

SECTION 3 | RETEACHING ACTIVITY
Measuring the Value of Trade

A. Making Inferences

The following questions deal with balance of trade. Answer them in the space provided.

1. Why is the foreign exchange market important to international trade?

_____

_____

2. What does a currency's rising value suggest about the demand for that currency? Why?

_____

_____

3. If the purchasing power of the U.S. dollar is greater than that of the Canadian dollar, what can you infer about the relative strength of the two currencies?

_____

_____

4. How did China succeed in creating a U.S. market for its exports? Explain.

_____

_____

5. Are the long-term effects of the U.S. trade balance with China more likely to be positive or negative? Explain your answer.

_____

_____

6. What factors led foreign investment in the United States to shift from a deficit in 1980 to a surplus in 2005?

_____

_____

CHAPTER 17

SECTION
4

RETEACHING ACTIVITY
Modern International Institutions

A. Comparing and Contrasting Economic Information

The following questions deal with international trade. Answer the questions in the space provided.

1. What are the advantages of NAFTA membership?

_____

2. What kinds of objections have been raised about NAFTA?

_____

3. What do developing countries gain by hosting multinationals?

_____

4. What are some potential disadvantages of hosting multinationals?

_____

B. Making Inferences

The following questions deal with international trade. Answer the questions in the space provided.

1. What trend do organizations such as the EU and MERCOSUR represent?

_____

2. How does the WTO reflect the growth of international trade?

_____

Copyright © McDougal Littell/Houghton Mifflin Company.

CHAPTER 17

**SECTION
1** | RETEACHING ACTIVITY
Definitions of Development

A. Explaining Economic Concepts

Find the term that best matches the description. Then write the letter of your answer on the line.

a. developed nations

b. less developed countries

c. infrastructure

d. transitional economies

e. per capita GDP

f. infant mortality rate

g. life expectancy

h. literacy rate

i. human development index

_____ **1.** Roads and other basic systems that support an economy

_____ **2.** Nations with a lower GDP, less industry, lower standard of living

_____ **3.** Countries that have moved or are moving from a command economy to a market economy

_____ **4.** Percentage of people older than 15 who can read and write

_____ **5.** Nations with a high GDP, industrialization, market economies, widespread private ownership, high standard of living

_____ **6.** Number of children who die within the first year of life per 1,000 live births

_____ **7.** Measures a country's real GDP against life expectancy and other social factors

_____ **8.** Average number of years a person can expect to live

_____ **9.** A nation's GDP divided by its total population

Copyright © McDougal Littell/Houghton Mifflin Company.

CHAPTER 18

CHAPTER 18

SECTION
2

RETEACHING ACTIVITY

A Framework for Economic Development Objectives

A. Comparing and Contrasting Economic Information

The following questions deal with the economic development of nations. Answer them in the space provided.

1. How are human capital and physical capital similar?

_____

_____

2. How is economic growth in a democracy most likely to be different from that in nations with other forms of government?

_____

_____

3. Why are investors more likely to invest in economies that demonstrate price stability?

_____

_____

4. Why are property rights less likely to be secure in less-developed nations?

_____

_____

5. In which country would you expect lower productivity, one that promotes equal opportunity for women or one that does not? Why?

_____

_____

6. How are debt restructuring and stabilization programs similar? How are they different?

_____

_____

_____

Copyright © McDougal Littell/Houghton Mifflin Company.

SECTION
3 | RETEACHING ACTIVITY
Economic Development Objectives

A. Analyzing Cause and Effect

The following questions deal with making the transition to a market economy. Answer them in the space provided.

1. How does an outdated infrastructure affect productivity and distribution?

   _____

   _____

2. Name a potential risk and a potential benefit resulting from the use of shock therapy on a nation's economy.

   _____

   _____

3. How has corruption slowed the development of Russia's market economy?

   _____

   _____

4. What caused an increase in China's light industry?

   _____

   _____

5. What effect have special economic zones had on China's GDP?

   _____

   _____

6. How does the removal of price supports affect prices?

   _____

   _____

Copyright © McDougal Littell/Houghton Mifflin Company.

CHAPTER 18

Answer Key

Copyright © McDougal Littell/Houghton Mifflin Company.

Unit 1 Benchmark Test

Part 1: Main Ideas

1. d
2. a
3. c
4. a
5. b
6. b
7. b
8. c
9. d
10. b
11. b
12. a
13. a
14. a
15. d
16. b
17. a
18. b
19. c
20. d
21. b
22. d

Part 2: Interpreting Charts

23. a
24. c
25. d

Unit 2 Benchmark Test

Part 1: Main Ideas

1. a
2. b
3. c
4. a
5. b
6. b
7. c
8. d
9. c
10. d
11. a
12. c
13. b

14. c
15. b
16. d
17. b
18. d
19. a
20. d
21. c
22. c

Part 2: Interpreting Graphs

23. b
24. a
25. d

Unit 3 Benchmark Test

Part 1: Main Ideas

1. d
2. a
3. b
4. c
5. a
6. d
7. a
8. c
9. a
10. a
11. d
12. c
13. b
14. b
15. a
16. a
17. c
18. a
19. a
20. b
21. b
22. c

Part 2: Interpreting Charts

23. c
24. a
25. b

Unit 4 Benchmark Test

Part 1: Main Ideas

1. b
2. a
3. c
4. a
5. c
6. b
7. d
8. b
9. d
10. b
11. d
12. b
13. c
14. c
15. b
16. b
17. c
18. c
19. d
20. d

Part 2: Interpreting Graphs

21. b
22. b
23. d
24. a
25. d

Unit 5 Benchmark Test

Part 1: Main Ideas

1. d
2. a
3. c
4. d
5. b
6. a
7. c
8. d
9. b
10. c
11. a
12. b
13. d

14. b
15. c
16. b
17. a
18. d
19. d
20. d
21. c

Part 2: Interpreting Documents

22. c
23. c

Part 3: Interpreting Advertisements

24. d
25. c

Unit 6 Benchmark Test

Part 1: Main Ideas

1. d
2. c
3. d
4. b
5. b
6. b
7. d
8. d
9. a
10. c
11. a
12. b
13. d
14. a
15. c
16. b
17. a
18. b
19. b
20. c
21. b
22. b

Part 2: Interpreting Charts

23. c
24. c
25. a

Unit 7 Benchmark Test

Part 1: Main Ideas

1. c
2. d
3. d
4. c
5. c
6. a
7. d
8. a
9. a
10. a
11. c
12. d
13. d
14. d
15. d
16. c
17. b
18. c
19. c
20. d
21. a

Part 2: Interpreting Graphs

22. a
23. a
24. a
25. a

Chapter 1

Section 1

Reteaching Activity

A. Comparing and Contrasting Economic Terms

1. Both are things that people acquire; needs are things people have to have to survive; wants are desires that people can satisfy by consuming goods and services.
2. Both are factors of production; land includes

all the natural resources found on or under the ground; capital includes all of the resources made and used by people to produce and distribute goods and services.
3. They are both factors of production; labor includes the human effort, time expended, and talent that goes into producing a good or a service; entrepreneurship includes vision, skills, and risk-taking required to create and run a business.
4. They both deal with a lack; in everyday speech, scarcity is a temporary shortage of something that people want or need; in economic terms, scarcity is a permanent situation for all people related to decisions about how to use scarce resources to satisfy unlimited wants.

B. Applying Economics Concepts

5. Question 1: What will be produced? , Example: Accept all reasonable examples.
6. Question 2: How will it be produced? , Example: Answers should relate to using natural and human resources.
7. Question 3: For whom will it be produced? , Example: Answers should relate to relate to government services or to the ability of people to pay for the goods and services from the private sector.

Copyright © McDougal Littell/Houghton Mifflin Company.

Chapter 1
Section 2
Reteaching Activity
A. Analyzing Economic Situations

1. Job A offers wages., Job B offers wages and future benefits., The opportunity cost of choosing job B is the loss in wages that you would have received from job A.

2. The utility of the individual pizzas is getting exactly what you want right now, including dessert., The utility of the extra large pizza is having a meal tomorrow as well as in tonight., The opportunity cost of choosing the individual pizzas is not having leftover pizza and having to make or buy lunch tomorrow.

3. The incentive for taking the high school course is that it is free., The incentive for taking the college course is that you may meet students who have similar aptitudes or interests; you may meet college staff who can help you with other math courses you need to take., Utility of the high school course and the college course are the same: to complete a requirement for taking future courses in college., Utility of the high school course and the college course are the same: to complete a requirement for taking future courses in

college., The opportunity cost of taking the high school course is having the money you would have earned by working full time at your job.

Chapter 1
Section 3
Reteaching Activity
A. Analyzing Economic Data

1. that only two types of products can be produced
2. 4,000 sets of flatware
3. 2,000 sets of flatware
4. Students should mark a point anywhere on the curve.
5. Students should label any point to the left of (or inside) the PPC.
6. It would shift to the right.

Chapter 1
Section 4
Reteaching Activity
A. Reviewing Economics Vocabulary

1. b
2. c
3. d
4. a

B. Identifying Economists' Tools

5. table
6. pie graph
7. economic model
8. line graph
9. bar graph
10. line graph

C. Summarizing the Accomplishments of an Important Economist

11. Student should summarize the model of the invisible hand in their own words and explain that this a foundation of modern economic policy and a rationale for free market economies.

Chapter 2
Section 1
Reteaching Activity
Comparing the Different Economic Systems

Traditional Economy: Description—Families, clans, or tribes make economic decisions based on customs and beliefs that have been handed down for generations. Survival is the main goal. Young people help with chores while learning their adult roles. The good of the group is always put above individual desires. Advantages—This type of economy clearly answers the three economic questions. There is little disagreement over economic goals because the decisions are made by custom. Disadvantages—These economies resist change, so they are generally less productive than they might be. Tradition and custom prevent people from taking on roles they are more suited, which

Copyright © McDougal Littell/Houghton Mifflin Company.

means the economy is less productive than it could be. The lower productivity and inefficiency of these economies means that people are less able to acquire wealth than they might be in other societies.

Command Economy:
Description—The government decides what will be produced, how it will be produced, and how it will be distributed among groups in society. Government officials consider the resources and needs of the entire country. The government usually owns the means of production. Advantages—Answers might include: the government's ability distribute resources equally among all different elements of society; the government working in the best interest of everyone in the country. Disadvantages—Answers might include: inefficiency based on erroneous government decisions; inefficiency based on unfair government decisions; inefficiency based on lack of motivation of people to work; lack of individual freedom.

Market Economy:
Description—The interactions between consumers and producers drive the economy. Producers decide which

goods or services they will offer, choosing how to use limited resources in ways they think will make them the most profits. Consumers are free to spend their money as they wish and to sell their labor to whomever they want. Consumers and producers both act in their own self-interest. Advantages—Answers might include: individual freedom to act in one's own self-interest; the most efficient use of resources because individuals not only act in their own self-interest, they also end up acting in the self-interest of others. Disadvantages: Answers might include: some individuals acting destructively toward themselves and toward others; uneven distribution of resources among different groups in society; some people's needs not being met, if they don't coincide with the way the majority of people meet those needs.

Chapter 2
Section 2
Reteaching Activity
A. Identifying Command Economic Systems

1. socialist; some of the major industries are owned by the government and the government provides essential services, including

education and health-care; however there is private ownership of a number of different economic factors including farmland, food distribution, and grocery stores.

2. communist; the government owns all of the factors of production and makes all of the major economic decisions, although there are democratic elements of government relating to how economic decisions are made.

3. socialist; the government owns the main industries of this country, but there is private ownership of other industries and services.

Chapter 2
Section 3
Reteaching Activity

1. product market
2. voluntary exchange
3. Specialization
4. capitalism
5. Competition
6. private property rights
7. factor market
8. profit
9. consumer sovereignty

Chapter 2
Section 4
Reteaching Activity
A. Using a Continuum to Describe Mixed Economies

1. Students should put the mark for this economy closer to the traditional end than to the command

Copyright © McDougal Littell/Houghton Mifflin Company.

end, since most people participate in the traditional aspects of the economy. However, the government's ownership of the coal mines and its possible plans for opening a state-run cannery would tend to the mark somewhere closer to the middle of the continuum.

2. Students should put the mark for this economy much closer to the market end than to the command end, since, except for public schools and public goods related to transportation, most of the factors of production are privately owned.

B. Analyzing and Evaluating Trends in Modern Economies

When a company goes from public to private ownership, people in foreign countries might made investments in the company. In this way, privatization and globalization can be linked.

4. Possible reasons include: the development of faster, cheaper, safer transportation; development of very fast, inexpensive, and easy financial transactions; development of numerous free trade agreements; the development of partnerships between companies in different countries. Students can list any of these. Most students will realize that the development of faster

and cheaper transportation for distributing goods and the development of fast, inexpensive, and easy financial transactions have been very important factors in the increase of globalization. Accept any student evaluation of the most important factor that includes reasons that are logical and well-expressed.

Chapter 3
Section 1
Reteaching Activity
A. Reviewing Economic Vocabulary

1. d
2. a
3. e
4. c
5. b
6. Free contract; legal equality; open opportunity.
7. Accept all rankings that students back with a logical explanation.
8. Other factors students might mention as being important in our economic system include legal protection of private property, access to education, and rule of law. Students might come up with other ideas, as well. Accept all evaluations and explanations that are clear and logical. You may wish to have students share their ideas and their answers in a class discussion.

Chapter 3
Section 2
Reteaching Activity
A. Summarizing Economic Roles

Consumers' Role: By choosing to buy certain products, consumers help determine what is profitable for producers and hence what will be produced in the near future. By choosing not to buy other products, consumers help producers what is not profitable to produce at that time. Producers tend to shift resources out of those products. Producers' Role: When a business is profitable, other producers notice. Many try to mimic or improve on a successful business by offering a similar product. This shifts resources toward a particular type of product that producers think will bring them profit. If a product becomes less profitable, producers tend to produce fewer of that product, shifting resources toward another product that is more profitable. Government's Role: Our government acts as both a consumer and producer. As a consumer, the government buys a variety of resources to help it run. As a producer, the government provides a wide variety of services.

Copyright © McDougal Littell/Houghton Mifflin Company.

B. Supporting Generalizations About our Economic System

1. Consumers "vote for" one product over a competing product by buying the product. Taken altogether, the products consumers favor are produced in higher quantities than those they do not favor
2. The U.S. economy is based on the free enterprise system. The government plays important roles in the economy by providing protections and by enacting regulations.
3. Local, state, and federal government agencies act as producers and consumers. Local, state, and federal government together employ about 16% of the labor force.
4. The government spends billions of dollars in both the product market and the factor market. The government spent about $2 trillion in 2005.

Chapter 3
Section 3

Reteaching Activity

1. safety net
2. free rider
3. infrastructure
4. market failure
5. transfer payment
6. positive externality
7. public good
8. public transfer payment
9. subsidy
10. negative externality

Chapter 4
Section 1
Reteaching Activity
A. Explaining Economic Concepts

1. Demand is the willingness to buy a good or service and the ability to pay for it
2. Answers should include the concept that a rise in price brings a drop in demand and vice versa.

C. Analyzing and Interpreting Data

3. It shows that as price goes down, the number demanded goes up
4. Students should realize that demand for movie tickets would be higher on a Saturday evening, when many people are off of work, than on Wednesday afternoon, when many people are at work. They should realize that demand for tickets at all prices would be lower on Wednesday afternoon; help the class realize that this general lowering of demand would mean that the demand curve would shift to the left.

Chapter 4
Section 2

National Council on Economic Education National Content Standards in Economics Reteaching Activity

A. Reviewing Economic Vocabulary

1. d
2. a
3. f
4. h
5. g
6. b
7. e
8. c

B. Restating Economic Ideas

Student answers should include the idea that the perceived benefit of using additional units of a good or service tend to go down over time as each unit is used.

Chapter 4
Section 3

Reteaching Activity

A. Reviewing Economic Concepts

1. a: a measure economists use to describe how responsive consumers are to price changes , b: when a change in price leads to a relatively larger change in the quantity demanded , c: when a change in price leads to a relatively smaller change in the quantity demanded , d: the situation in which the

Copyright © McDougal Littell/Houghton Mifflin Company.

percentage change in price and the percentage change in quantity demanded are equal

2. a: If substitutes are available, demand tends to be elastic; if substitutes are not available, demand tends to be inelastic., b: If a person spends a relatively large proportion of income on a nonessential good or service, the demand tends to be elastic; if the person spends a relatively small proportion of income on the good, demand tends to be inelastic, c: If a product is a necessity, demand for it tends to be inelastic; if it is a luxury, demand for it tends to be inelastic.

B. Applying Economic Concepts

3. a. (200 – 310) / 200 = 110 / 200 x 100 = 55% ($5.99 – $3.99) / $5.99 = $2.00 / $5.99 x 100 = 33% 55% / 33% = 1.66, which is greater than 1, so demand is elastic, b. 200 x $5.99 = $1,198.00 310 x $3.99 = $1,236.90 Total revenue is greater when the price is lowered; therefore demand is elastic.

Chapter 5

Section 1

Reteaching Activity

A. Reviewing Economic Concepts

1. supply
2. rises
3. falls

B. Restating and Interpreting Economic Data

4. 2,000
5. $5.00
6. 1,600
7. $4.00
8. 1,200
9. $3.00
10. 800
11. $2.00
12. 400
13. $1.00

14. It shows that as the price rises, the number of cards the producer is willing to supply rises and that as the price falls, the number of cards the producer is willing to supply falls.

15. They probably make more profit on more expensive cards; the additional profit motivates producers to supply more cards.

Chapter 5

Section 2

Reteaching Activity

A. Identifying Economic Data

1. Number of workers
2. Total product
3. Total cost
4. Marginal cost
5. Marginal revenue
6. Total revenue
7. Profit
8. $660.00
9. $372.00

B. Interpreting Economic Data

10. 110 centerpieces; with between four and six workers, each new worker causes the total output of

centerpieces to grow, but at a decreasing rate

11. The profits start to decline. This may occur because the workspace becomes too crowded, the workers can't organize their work efficiently, the workers socialize more, there are conflicts with personalities. Accept other reasons that make sense.

12. 128 centerpieces; at this point marginal cost and marginal revenue are equal, and the business is making its highest level of profits. Five workers are employed.

13. With seven workers, the store experiences negative returns. Seven workers make fewer centerpieces than six workers do.

Chapter 5

Section 3

Reteaching Activity

Classifying Economic Factors and Applying Economic Concepts

1. technology; supply will increase
2. government action; supply of tobacco will decrease; supply of corn will increase
3. productivity; supply will increase
4. change in number of producers; supply will increase
5. change in producer expectation; supply will decrease
6. input costs; supply will decrease

Copyright © McDougal Littell/Houghton Mifflin Company.

7. change in producer expectation; supply will increase

Chapter 5
Section 4
Reteaching Activity

A.

1. It is a measure of how responsive producers are to changes in price.

2. true

3. Supply is inelastic if a 15 percent rise in price causes an increase in quantity supplied that is less than 15 percent. –or—Supply is inelastic if a 15 percent drop in price causes a decrease in quantity supplied that is less than 15 percent. –or-- Supply is elastic if a 15 percent drop in price causes a decrease quantity supplied that is greater than 15 percent.

4. The supply curve of an item that has an elastic supply is more gradual/shallower than the supply curve of an item that has an inelastic supply. –or—The supply curve of an item that has an inelastic supply is steeper than the supply curve of an item that has an elastic supply.

5. true

B. Explaining Economic Concepts

6. Students might name such items as yearly crops or items produced from yearly crops, items that depend on some kind of processing

which requires equipment that limits how much can be processed, and items that require a lot of equipment or complex technology to manufacture. Students should explain what limits the ability of suppliers to quickly increase supply.

7. $4.00 - $2.50 = $1.50 = .375 x 100 =37.5% $4.00 $4.00 3000 – 2500 = 500 = .1666 x 100 = 16.6% 3000 3000 Supply is inelastic because a 37.5% drop in price cause only a 16.6% drop in supply

Chapter 6
Section 1
Reteaching Activity

B. Analyzing and Interpreting Data

1. a. Students should circle the point where the supply curve and the demand curve intersect. b. $0.35 per toothbrush

2. A surplus; the producer would supply 3,250 toothbrushes at that prices, but dentists would only demand 1,750 toothbrushes at that price, causing a surplus of 1,500 toothbrushes.

3. A shortage; dentists would demand 3,500 toothbrushes at that price, but producers would only make 1,000 toothbrushes, causing a shortage of 2,500 toothbrushes.

4. a. Students should draw arrows on their graph to

show that the supply curve would move to the right. b. The equilibrium price would go down.

Chapter 6
Section 2
Reteaching Activity

A. Categorizing Situations Using Economic Concepts

1. flexibility
2. independence
3. efficiency
4. equality

B. Explaining Economic Concepts

5. a drop in price; or not a good time
6. true
7. raise prices; or a surplus occurs

Chapter 6
Section 3
Reteaching Activity

1. rationing
2. price floor
3. black market
4. minimum wage
5. price ceiling
6. minimum wage, price floor

B. Comparing and Contrasting Economic Concepts

price floor: above the equilibrium price; results in a surplus; answers will vary, but should be similar to the minimum wage (Congress sets minimum price for pizzas at $50—millions of high school students face starvation)

Copyright © McDougal Littell/Houghton Mifflin Company.

price ceiling: below the equilibrium price; results in a shortage; answers will vary, but should be similar to rent control (New law forces auto makers to sell sports coupes for $50—rioting results when dealerships run out of cars)

Chapter 7
Section 1
Reteaching Activity
A. Finding Main Ideas

1. standardized product
2. price taker
3. imperfect competition
4. market structure
5. perfect competition

B. Making Inferences

6. Yes. They are independent because they do not work together to influence prices. They are well informed because buyers can comparison shop. Sellers can learn what their competition is charging.
7. Many buyers and sellers; buyers and sellers are free to enter and exit market.
8. Standardized product.

Chapter 7
Section 2
Reteaching Activity
Explaining Economic Concepts

1. j
2. d
3. g
4. i
5. f
6. a

7. c
8. e
9. b
10. h

Chapter 7
Section 3
Reteaching Activity
Comparing and Contrasting Economic Information

1. true
2. An oligopoly has many buyers and few sellers.
3. Standardized products are characteristic of perfect competition and industrial oligolpolies; OR Differentiated products are characteristic of monopolistic competition.
4. true
5. About half of the manufacturing industries in the United States are oligopolistic.
6. true
7. true
8. Start-up costs to enter a monopolistic competition market are less than those for entry into an oligopolistic market.

Chapter 7
Section 4
Reteaching Activity
Generalizing from Economic Information

1. Trusts could control prices and output.
2. the power to control and break up monopolies

3. to enforce antitrust legislation
4. when a company is engaged in unfair business practices
5. to ensure that consumers have adequate information about a product or service

1. Possible answer: The government creates laws and sets up agencies to promote competition and to protect the consumer from unfair business practices.

Chapter 8
Section 1
Reteaching Activity

1. a business owned and controlled by one person
2. by producing goods and services that provide what consumers want
3. securing a place to do business, raising money to finance start-up expenses, such as rent and inventory, and meeting legal requirements, such as obtaining a business license
4. easy to open or close, few regulations, freedom and control, owner keeps profits
5. The proprietor might have to go into personal debt to pay off business debts.
6. limited funds and limited life

Copyright © McDougal Littell/Houghton Mifflin Company.

Chapter 8

Section 2

Reteaching Activity

Conducting Marginal Cost-Marginal Benefit Analysis

1. Graphic Organizer: Decision To Be Made: whether to form a partnership; Added Costs: potential for disagreements, unlimited liability, limited life, possibility of straining the friendship; Added Benefits: easy set-up, greater resources, possibility of specializing, easy to dissolve, few government regulations; Decision: Answers will vary. Students may decide to form, or not to form, the partnership.

1. Answers will vary. Those choosing to form the partnership may say that there were more advantages than disadvantages. Those choosing not to form the partnership may say that the disadvantages outweighed the benefits or that they did not wish to jeopardize their friendship.

Chapter 8

Section 3

Reteaching Activity

Comparing and Contrasting Economic Information

1. true
2. stocks
3. true

4. horizontal
5. multinational corporation

Chapter 8

Section 4

Reteaching Activity

A. Making Inferences

1. a. Franchisees pay the parent company in return for the right to sell the company's products., b. A franchisee runs an individual business but receives assistance and direction from the parent company.

2. a. One benefit of a franchise is training provided by the parent company., b. Additional benefits include proven products, common décor, and paid advertising.

3. a. One disadvantage is initial cost, as purchasing a franchise is expensive., b. Other disadvantages are having to share profits with the franchiser, and having to follow the franchiser's operating rules.

4. a. Consumer co-ops keep prices low for their members., b. Producer cooperatives ensure more efficient processing or better marketing; or credit unions may provide health insurance at a reduced price.

5. a. Some nonprofits, such as the American Red Cross, are organized for the benefit of society., b. Some nonprofits,

such as the American Bar Association, are professional organizations that exist to promote the common interests of their members.

6. a. A nonprofit, like a corporation, must receive a government charter. , b. A nonprofit, like a corporation, has unlimited life.

Chapter 9

Section 1

Reteaching Activity

Analyzing Cause and Effect

1. Highly skilled workers receive higher pay.
2. discrimination
3. Women, minorities not promoted.
4. Governments enact minimum wage laws.
5. Employers offer high wages to attract workers.
6. occupational segregation (Women are more likely to fill lower-paying jobs such as nurse, teacher.)

Chapter 9

Section 2

Reteaching Activity

A. Making Inferences

1. a. Job opportunities for women have improved. b. During the second half of the 20th century, women have entered the labor force at a faster rate than men.

2. a. About 30 percent of workers have a college degree. b. About 30

Copyright © McDougal Littell/Houghton Mifflin Company.

Economics: Concepts and Choices

percent of U.S. workers have some college credits.

3. a. U.S. businesses hire other firms both in the United States and abroad to provide goods or services. b. Foreign countries practice insourcing by bringing jobs to the United States.

4. a. Service jobs have increased 26 percent since 1950. b. The ten fastest-growing occupations are service-related.

5. a. More than 80 percent of managers and professionals use a computer at work. b. The Internet and laptop computers enable workers to telecommute.

6. a. Contingent employees lower labor costs, as most do not receive benefits. b. Part-time workers offer employers greater flexibility. b. Part-time workers offer employers greater flexibility.

Chapter 9
Section 3
Reteaching Activity

A. Drawing Conclusions

Conclusion: The strength of labor unions has been seriously weakened. Fact: Right-to-work laws favor businesses rather than unions. Fact: Unions are less likely to press for higher wages, as pay cuts and loss of benefits have become more common.

Fact: Unions strike less often for fear that employers will replace workers or close plants.

B. Clarifying

7. collective bargaining
8. union shop
9. industrial union
10. closed shop
11. craft union

Chapter 10
Section 1
Reteaching Activity

A. Explaining Economic Concepts

1. barter
2. standard of value
3. commodity money
4. currency
5. fiat money
6. demand deposits
7. representative money
8. near money
9. store of value
10. medium of exchange

Chapter 10
Section 2
Reteaching Activity

A. Making Inferences

1. No, because many banks issued their own currency and did not back it up with gold or silver.
2. Hamilton believed that the federal government had the authority to create a national bank that would regulate currency. His efforts resulted in the chartering of the country's first national bank.

3. Opposition to the bank was so strong that Congress refused to renew its charter. As a result, state banks increased the money supply, causing inflation.
4. Yes, because it caused him to veto the charter of the Second Bank of the United States. With no federal oversight, state banks engaged in questionable practices that led to economic instability.
5. Roosevelt hoped to put the economy back on its feet and avoid further financial panic.
6. Deregulation enabled S&Ls to take more risks, causing many to fail. Depositors lost money and billions of dollars of taxpayers' money were spent to restructure the S&L industry.

Chapter 10
Section 3
Reteaching Activity

Chapter 11
Section 1
Reteaching Activity

Explaining Economic Concepts

1. f
2. b
3. d
4. i
5. h
6. a
7. e
8. j
9. g

Copyright © McDougal Littell/Houghton Mifflin Company.

10. c

Chapter 11

Section 2

Reteaching Activity

A. Applying Economic Concepts

1. true
2. true
3. interest
4. Short-term
5. true
6. diversification
7. more
8. true

Chapter 11

Section 3

Reteaching Activity

A. Comparing and Contrasting Economic Information

1. The Dow peaked in May 2006; the NASDAQ also peaked in May 2006.
2. Both indexes reached their lowest point in October 2005.
3. They are very similar.
4. Stocks on the Dow represent the economy's most important sectors. NASDAQ stocks are primarily issued by companies involved in technology.
5. Over the counter trading, made possible by a centralized computer system.

Chapter 11

Section 4

Reteaching Activity

A. Analyzing Economic Data

1. BBB-rated bonds
2. about .5 percent
3. 25 percent
4. BBB-rated bonds, because they have a lesser rating than the AAA bonds
5. They would be more likely to buy AAA, because they may be purchased to mature in 25 years. The longest maturity for BBB-rated bonds is 20 years.
6. Both curves increase. The curve for AAA-rated bonds is flatter, extends over an additional 5 years, and shows a lower yield.

Chapter 12

Section 1

Reteaching Activity

A. Explaining Economic Concepts

Organizer: consumption, investment, government spending, net exports

B. Explaining Economic Concepts

1. real GDP
2. underground economy, nonmarket activities
3. gross national product, or GNP
4. net national product, or NNP
5. national income, or NI

Chapter 12

Section 2

Reteaching Activity

A. Explaining Economic Concepts

1. f
2. c
3. b
4. d
5. h
6. g
7. a
8. d
9. i
10. e

Chapter 12

Section 3

Reteaching Activity

Making Inferences

1. quality of labor
2. technological innovation
3. energy costs
4. financial markets
5. Well-educated and healthy workers are more productive.
6. New inventions and better ways of doing things improve productivity; they help workers to be more efficient; information technology has increased productivity by allowing greater and faster access to information.
7. Reduced energy costs increase productivity by allowing factories and businesses to lower production costs; increased energy costs reduce productivity.

Copyright © McDougal Littell/Houghton Mifflin Company.

8. Financial markets improve productivity by moving money where it is needed; lack of financial markets or inefficient markets reduce productivity.

Chapter 13

Section 1

Reteaching Activity

A. Classifying Types of Unemployment

1. structural
2. frictional
3. structural
4. seasonal
5. frictional

B. Explaining Economic Concepts

6. An underemployed worker has a job, but it either doesn't provide enough hours for the worker or doesn't employ skills the worker has. An unemployed worker has no job and is looking for work.

7. During full employment, no unemployment is caused by decreased economic activity. Frictional unemployment is the main type of unemployment workers experience during a period of full employment.

Chapter 13

Section 2

Reteaching Activity

A. Reviewing Economic Vocabulary

1. e

2. a
3. c
4. f
5. b
6. g
7. d

B. Describing Causes of Poverty

8. Single-parent families are more likely to struggle financially than two-parent families.

9. Women and minorities are more likely to face wage discrimination and be segregated in low-paying jobs than are white males.

10. With many manufacturing jobs outsourced to Mexico, Central America, or overseas, there are fewer higher paying jobs for low-skilled workers; this means that people with low levels of skill are more likely to earn low wages and to be at risk for poverty.

Chapter 13

Section 3

Reteaching Activity

A. Reviewing Economic Vocabulary

1. h
2. b
3. d
4. i
5. k
6. g
7. j
8. a
9. f
10. e
11. c

Chapter 14

Section 1

Reteaching Activity

A. Classifying Principles of and Criteria for Taxation

1. benefit-received
2. simplicity or efficiency
3. equity
4. ability-to-pay and equity
5. efficiency

B. Explaining Economic Concepts

6. F; With a proportional tax, or a flat tax, the rate is the same for all taxpayers. OR With a progressive tax, the tax rate depends on income.

7. T
8. T

Chapter 14

Section 2

Reteaching Activity

A. Reviewing Different Kinds of Federal Taxes

1. INDIVIDUAL INCOME TAX: Description—Tax on income individuals earn; collected mainly through withholding; indexing prevents tax increases due solely to inflation / Tax structure—progressive / Who pays—anyone who earns income in the U.S. / Tax rate—10% at the lowest income levels up to 35% at the highest income levels / Percent of federal revenue it raises—45% // SOCIAL SECURITY TAX: Description—Tax on income individuals earn; collected mainly through

Copyright © McDougal Littell/Houghton Mifflin Company.

withholding; income not taxed after about $95,000; raised to pay for Social Security benefits for the elderly and for people in families who have lost wage earners / Tax structure—proportional/regressive / Who pays—Anyone who earns income in the U.S. and his or her employer / Tax rate—6.2% of employee's income paid by employee; 6.2% of employee's income paid by employer / Percent of federal revenue it raises—part of FICA, which raises 37% // MEDICARE TAX: Description—Tax on income individuals earn; collected mainly through withholding; goes to pay for medical expenses for the elderly / Tax structure—proportional / Who pays—Anyone who earns income in the U.S. and his or her employer / Tax rate—1.45% of employee's income paid by employee; 1.45% of employee's income paid by employer / Percent of federal revenue it raises—part of FICA, which raises 37% // UNEMPLOYMENT TAX: Description—Tax on income of individuals up to the first $7,000 the person earns / Tax structure—proportional / Who pays—all employers / Tax rate—X / Percent of federal revenue it raises—part of FICA,

which raises 37% // CORPORATE INCOME TAX: Description—Tax on corporate profits; proportion of revenue the federal government has gotten from corporate income taxes has dropped from 275% in 1950 to 9.6% in 2007 / Tax structure—proportional / Who pays—8% of U.S. corporations / Tax rate—35% / Percent of federal revenue it raises—11% // ESTATE TAX: Description—Tax on the assets of a person who has died if the estate is valued at more than $2 million / Tax structure—X / Who pays—X / Tax rate—X / Percent of federal revenue it raises—less than 1% // GIFT TAX: Description—Tax on gifts a person gives to a non-family member, or a family member above a certain amount / Tax structure—X / Who pays—X / Tax rate—X / Percent of federal revenue it raises—less than 1% // EXCISE TAX: Description—Tax on particular goods or services; examples include gasoline and telephone service/ Tax structure—X / Who pays—X / Tax rate—X / Percent of federal revenue it raises—3% // CUSTOMS DUTIES: Description—Tax on goods imported into the United States; also called tariffs; have been decreasing in

the past few decades / Tax structure—X / Who pays—X / Tax rate—X / Percent of federal revenue it raises—1% // USER FEES: Description—Fees people pay when they use a particular public good; entrance fees to national parks are examples // Tax structure—X / Who pays—the people using the public good / Tax rate—X / Percent of federal revenue it raises—less than 2%

Chapter 14
Section 3
Reteaching Activity
A. Reviewing Economics Vocabulary

Discretionary spending, allocations, Mandatory spending, entitlement, Medicare, Medicaid, Social Security, federal budget, grant-in-aid, resource allocation, redistribution of income

Chapter 14
Section 4
Reteaching Activity
A. Analyzing Economic Information

1. local government; 2%
2. intergovernmental revenue, other
3. property tax
4. state government

B. Determining Which Level of Government Is Most Likely to Make an Expenditure

5. local

Copyright © McDougal Littell/Houghton Mifflin Company.

6. state
7. state
8. local
9. local

Chapter 15
Section 1
Reteaching Activity

A. Categorizing Fiscal Policy Tools

1. automatic stabilizer; progressive income taxes
2. discretionary fiscal policy; contractionary
3. discretionary fiscal policy; expansionary
4. automatic stabilizer; public transfer payments
5. discretionary fiscal policy; expansionary
6. discretionary fiscal policy; contractionary
7. discretionary fiscal policy; contractionary

Chapter 15
Section 2
Reteaching Activity

A. Distinguishing Fact from Opinion

1. O; facts can relate what role the government takes in the nation's economy.
2. F; opinions can relate to whether it is easy or difficult to determine whether a specific tax rate is high or low.
3. F; opinions can relate to whether tax cuts for businesses or government spending would be a better way to address an economic slowdown.

4. O; facts can relate to John Maynard Keynes, who promoted this idea, or to the evidence that this policy worked in the late 1930s and the 1940s.
5. O; facts can relate to what government regulations are or to any evidence that they increase, have no effect on, or decrease business profits.
6. F; opinions can relate to the effectiveness of Keynes's policies.
7. F; opinions can relate to whether governments should institute such programs in the first place or to any other aspect of the role of the government in the economy.

B. Designing a Poster

Posters should include a central image and a slogan, with a fact or explanation supporting it. Accept all designs that include an accurate portrayal of some aspect of either demand-side or supply-side economic policy and its goals.

Chapter 15
Section 3
Reteaching Activity

1. deficit spending
2. budget surplus
3. balanced budget
4. budget deficit
5. national debt

B. Analyzing Causes and Effects

6. 6. national emergencies, including weather-related emergencies or wars
7. 7. the need for public goods and services, including infrastructure
8. 8. stabilization of the economy through expansionary fiscal policy
9. 9. the governmental role of taking care of elderly people and helping people deal with the effects of poverty
10. 10. stimulating the economy and improving public infrastructure through government spending
11. 11. raising interest rates through the crowding-out effect, which causes economic slowdowns
12. 12. creating such a large debt burden that the government requires increased revenues through higher taxes, which causes economic slowdowns

Chapter 16
Section 1
Reteaching Activity

A. Explaining Economic Concepts

1. To stablize the U.S. financial system by creating a central bank.
2. The Fed provides regulation and oversight.
3. It can lend large sums of money.

Copyright © McDougal Littell/Houghton Mifflin Company.

4. The Fed is an independent organization within the government.
5. Because it provides banking services to other banks.
6. One that is both national and regional.
7. The Board supervises the Fed's operations and sets policy.
8. Nationally chartered banks are automatically members. State-chartered banks may apply for membership.

Chapter 16

Section 2

Reteaching Activity

A. Applying Economic Concepts

1. The bank might ask the Fed for a loan, which would be necessary because the local economy is seasonal.
2. The Fed serves as a clearinghouse for checks.
3. The Fed conducts bank exams to be sure that banks are not involved in risky practices.
4. The Fed holds money the federal government receives from taxes. These are the government's "deposits." The Social Security payment is similar to a withdrawal an individual makes from a bank account.
5. Increasing the RRR decreases a bank's ability to create money because the bank must put a higher percentage of its money in reserve funds. It therefore

has less money to lend so that less money can be created.
6. The Fed manages the supply of money. It therefore needs to know how much money individuals and businesses need. Income level is one factor that helps to provide that information.

Chapter 16

Section 3

Reteaching Activity

A. Explaining Economic Concepts

1. i
2. d
3. e
4. b
5. a
6. f
7. j
8. g
9. h
10. c

Chapter 16

Section 4

Reteaching Activity

A. Analyzing Cause and Effect

1. During periods of economic stagnation; to increase the money supply and increase aggregate demand.
2. The Fed buys bonds on the open market to expand the money supply and stimulate the economy. It sells bonds to tighten the money supply and slow economic growth.

3. Poor timing may disrupt the business cycle and make an economic problem worse.
4. To decrease the money supply; during periods of inflation or rapid economic growth.
5. As a result of expansionary policies, real GDP increases. As a result of contractionary policies, it decreases.
6. Yes. When economic policies are not coordinated, they work against each other.

Chapter 17

Section 1

Reteaching Activity

A. Finding Main Ideas

1. Yes, because it enables nations to trade products that are efficiently made and for which they receive increased profit.
2. It limits the number of products that a nation produces. Nations depend on other nations to provide products that they do not produce.
3. When it can make a product more efficiently.
4. When it can make a product at a lower opportunity cost.
5. Nations increase their production ratios and economic growth. They can acquire goods and services they cannot produce. They can acquire technology and expertise needed to grow economically.

Copyright © McDougal Littell/Houghton Mifflin Company.

6. Exports reduce supply and increase price.

7. They are motivated to become more efficient.

8. Trade may cause jobs to increase in some sectors and decrease in others.

Chapter 17

Section 2

Reteaching Activity

A. Explaining Economic Concepts

1. trade barrier
2. quota
3. tariff
4. voluntary export restraint
5. embargo
6. dumping
7. revenue tariffs
8. protective tariffs
9. trade war
10. protectionism

Chapter 17

Section 3

Reteaching Activity

A. Making Inferences

1. Without it, buyers and sellers would have no system for exchanging currency.

2. The demand is increasing, because demand causes an increase in price.

3. The U.S. currency is stronger than the Canadian currency.

4. It pegged the RenMinBi to the dollar so that its value would remain weak relative to the dollar. The stronger dollar has led the U.S. to

purchase large quantities of "cheap" Chinese goods.

5. They are more likely to be negative because the U.S. may be forced to borrow, sell assets, or tap into foreign reserves to pay off the debt.

6. The economy became more stable and inflation attained relatively low levels.

Chapter 17

Section 4

Reteaching Activity

A. Comparing and Contrasting Economic Information

1. Specialization, increased efficiency, competitive advantage over the EU and Japan, expanded markets, new jobs

2. Objections have been political, social, and environmental.

3. Jobs and technology

4. Unfair treatment of workers; multinationals may gain too much political power.

B. Making Inferences

1. The formation of regional customs unions and free trade zones.

2. International trade has become so common that it requires oversight and regulation, which the WTO provides. Its large membership of 149 nations also reflects the growth of international trade.

Chapter 18

Section 1

Reteaching Activity

A. Explaining Economic Concepts

1. c
2. b
3. d
4. h
5. a
6. f
7. i
8. g
9. e

Chapter 18

Section 2

Reteaching Activity

A. Comparing and Contrasting Economic Information

1. Both are necessary for increased productivity, efficiency, and economic growth.

2. Economic growth is greater in a democracy.

3. Price stability makes the economy more predictable.

4. Favoritism and corruption make property rights less secure.

5. One that promotes equality, because women can develop their skills and participate fully in the labor force.

6. Both are designed to assist developing nations. Debt restructuring assists nations to obtain more favorable terms for repayment of debts. Stabilization programs are designed to steady a nation's economy

Copyright © McDougal Littell/Houghton Mifflin Company.

by overseeing economic
activities such as reducing
foreign trade deficit and
external debt.

Chapter 18

Section 3

Reteaching Activity

A. Analyzing Cause and Effect

1. It limits productivity and distribution.
2. A potential risk is excessive inflation. A potential benefit is a quick transition to a market economy.
3. Corruption has given some businesses an unfair advantage, thereby limiting competition.
4. The decision of many localities to invest in it.
5. They have helped to increase it substantially.
6. It causes them to rise and often to become inflationary.

Copyright © McDougal Littell/Houghton Mifflin Company.